Business Cases in

Statistical Decision Making

Computer Based Applications

Lawrence H. Peters
Texas Christian University

J. Brian Gray
University of Alabama

Prentice Hall, Englewood Cliffs, New Jersey 07632

Library of Congress Cataloging-in-Publication Data

PETERS, LAWRENCE H.
Business cases in statistical decision making : computer based applications / LAWRENCE H. PETERS, J. BRIAN GRAY.
  p. cm.
  Includes bibliographical references and index.
  ISBN 0-13-285834-7
  1. Industrial management—statistical methods—Case studies.
2. Commercial statistics—Case studies. I. Gray, J. Brian.
II. Title
HD30.215.P47 1994
658′.0072—dc20   93-5828

Acquisitions editor: Valerie Ashton
Editorial/production supervision: Edie Riker
Production coordinator: Trudy Pisciotti

© 1994 by Lawrence H. Peters and J. Brian Gray
Published by Prentice-Hall, Inc.
A Paramount Communications Company
Englewood Cliffs, New Jersey 07632

Printed in the United States of America

10 9 8 7 6 5 4 3 2 1

Minitab is a registered trademark of Minitab, Inc., 3081 Enterprise Drive, State College, PA
    16801-3008 (Phone: 814-238-3280 Fax: 814-238-4383).
Execustat is a registered trademark of Strategy Graphics, Inc.
Systat is a registered trademark of Systat, Inc.
Microsoft Excel is a registered trademark of Microsoft Corporation.
Harvard Graphics is a registered trademark of Software Publication Corporation.

ISBN   0-13-285834-7

Prentice-Hall International (UK) Limited, *London*
Prentice-Hall of Australia Pty. Limited, *Sydney*
Prentice-Hall Canada Inc., *Toronto*
Prentice-Hall Hispanoamericana, S.A., *Mexico*
Prentice-Hall of India Private Limited, *New Delhi*
Prentice-Hall of Japan, Inc., *Tokyo*
Simon & Schuster Asia Pte. Ltd., *Singapore*
Editora Prentice-Hall do Brasil, Ltda., *Rio de Janeiro*

Table of Contents

Preface

This book is dedicated to students. Our experiences with them helped us understand that a course in business statistics needs to be more than formulas and problem sets. They clarified our need to demonstrate that a course in statistics is a vital part of the business curriculum. They helped us see how we could translate their needs into a teaching methodology that meets academic goals and to do so in a way that is both interesting and challenging, and which clarifies to students that statistical reasoning is a powerful business tool. We thank them for opening our minds to creating cases where the goal is not to get the right statistical result, but to make good business decisions.

We know from experience that the "hands-on" case approach helps to insure that students not only learn statistics, but retain key ideas and actually recognize how and when to apply statistical reasoning in solving problems. Some of the cases have been used successfully during mass lectures to 300 undergraduate business students to motivate discussions about problems in real business settings that require statistical analysis as part of the decision-making process. Most of the cases were assigned as group projects to a hardworking class of MBA students during the Fall 1992 Semester at the University of Alabama. Their high level of interest and involvement in solving the cases, as well as the outstanding analyses and well-written reports that they produced, convinced us that the case approach can be extremely valuable in teaching business statistics. In addition to learning a statistical computing package, these MBA students gained a great deal of experience with other computer tools (such as spreadsheets, presentation graphics packages, and color printers) and small group dynamics. We owe these students a debt of gratitude for their useful feedback.

Our thanks go to Karen Zikos, our sales representative at Prentice Hall, for listening to our ideas, and to Valerie Ashton, our editor at Prentice Hall, for her willingness to give us the opportunity to try our ideas about using cases in business statistics courses. We are grateful for Valerie's faith in our methodology and in our ability to produce it in book form. Special thanks to Beth Solt of the Author Assistance Program at Minitab, Inc. for providing us with the Minitab Statistical Software package which was used to produce the computer output shown in our *Instructor's Guide*. We also want to thank Todd Baumgartner and Eddie Erdmann, our student assistants, for their help on this project. Their feedback from trying out the cases on various statistical software packages is greatly appreciated. We also would like to thank our families, especially Jennifer and Anne, for their support and encouragement as we worked on this labor of love.

Lawrence H. Peters

J. Brian Gray

Introduction

All business statistics courses require students to work on "problem sets." The goal of each problem is to have students perform a statistical computation or to apply a prescribed statistical tool to a small set of data in order to come up with "the right answer." Such problems may or may not be given a managerial or business context which generates the numerical data students must analyze. Even in those instances in which problem sets are described in a business context, the goal, nonetheless, is to have students apply specified statistical procedures in order to come up with the correct numerical answer or statistical summary.

We believe that an emphasis on "getting the right answer" falls short of the important contribution that statistical knowledge can provide. When we ask our students to get the right answer, they fail to understand why and how statistical knowledge can be useful. They fail to understand how this knowledge can help them make better decisions in real business situations. Failing to clarify the value of statistical knowledge, therefore, can leave the student questioning the relevance of their course work in this area.

Business Cases in Statistical Decision Making was developed specifically in response to this issue. It addresses a current need discussed repeatedly over the past several years by leading business statistics educators at the "Making Statistics More Effective in Schools of Business" national conferences held annually since 1986. (See Easton, G. E., Roberts, H. V., and Tiao, G. C. (1988), "Making Statistics More Effective in Schools of Business," *Journal of Business and Economic Statistics*, 6, 247-260 for a report from the first conference.) One consistently mentioned

1

and strongly endorsed idea resulting from these conferences is the need to engage the student's interest through the use of real business applications. These educators underscored the importance of showing students the range of real-world problems in which statistical understanding is valuable — in short, why and how statistical knowledge can be useful. Our overriding goal in preparing this case book was to help students understand how statistics can be useful for solving commonly observed managerial and business problems, thus helping students appreciate why course work in business statistics is relevant to their future professional business careers.

In contrast to "problem sets," like those typically found at the end of each chapter in a statistics book, this discussion implies that the goal of a statistical analysis is not just to get the right answer. Rather, the goal is to correctly understand a business situation, solve a real problem, and make a good decision. To this end, students will be required to identify relevant variables, choose an appropriate analysis plan, produce correct results (remember, this is the sole goal of the typical problem set), interpret their findings and make recommendations regarding the managerial/business issues presented to them. Obviously, getting the right answer is necessary in order to meet these business objectives. But, the emphasis is on the business objective and, as such, it is hoped that students will begin to see the relevance of their study of business statistics.

In addition, these statistics educators pointed to the case method as the ideal way to provide college students with such an understanding. There would appear to be endless numbers of important issues, problems and decisions in business situations that are best resolved by appropriately analyzing and interpreting data. These issues, problems and decisions are, in turn, best taught by presenting students with a description of a business situation and then involving them in the thought process that produces an educated and sound business decision. The case method is ideally suited for such problems.

In all areas of business, many key issues, problems and decisions involve the identification and examination of additional information (*i.e.,* data), beyond that found in the written case. Issues related to choosing the most appropriate channels for advertising, for choosing the least expensive but most effective business solution, for selecting personnel for an important job, for identifying key new business strategies, for deciding how scarce resources are best spent, and so forth all involve identifying and collecting appropriate information and then using that information properly in order to arrive at an effective solution.

We designed this case book to give students an opportunity to work on a set of representative real-world business problems that require the identification and appropriate use of additional information. These cases specifically require students to "go to the data" as a basis for defining the problem, developing alternative courses of action and/or suggesting meaningful solutions. We think that such a process not only makes the cases more "life-like," but, in addition, teaches students several additional important lessons along the way. For example:

1. Students should begin to appreciate (maybe for the first time) how simple statistical procedures can be applied to solve "life-like" problems. There is a reason for having to take statistics courses — appropriately used and interpreted, statistical analysis increases our ability to make and implement better managerial and business decisions. Statistical reasoning is one of the most important tools that a business person can have. It's better to learn that lesson now, before being faced with that first real decision to be made and ending up falling back on intuition when a good analytical solution is possible.

2. Students should begin to appreciate the importance of keeping relevant information for making business decisions and, if need be, as a basis for defending those decisions to others (*e.g.*, their supervisors, their customers, governmental agencies, or courts).

3. As a more specific example of the second point, students will have the opportunity to work with, and see the value of, computerized data files. Such experience, even in the limited context provided by this case book, is important given the growing recognition for the value of computerized information systems in modern organizations.

4. Students will receive hands-on experience using the computer as a tool for solving business problems. Without argument, such experience is regarded as a valuable part of the modern business curriculum. Learning how to use the computer as a tool for decision making and problem solving, as opposed to learning how to

program, requires practice — practice not aimed at making the computer do things, but practice aimed at having the computer help students think through problems and make better decisions.

5. Students will receive the benefit of learning how to use a statistical software package (chosen by their instructor). Becoming familiar with a business statistical software package is the first step in making the computer fulfill its promise of helping to make better managerial and business decisions. Basic familiarity with software, regardless of the particular program used, will increase the comfort level of students for working with statistical packages in general, and hopefully pique students' interest in their use in the future.

Combined with learning how to "think statistically" and seeing how statistics can be an important business tool, the use of PC's and statistical software will start students on the way to developing relevant computer literacy skills that can be applied in many work settings. Use of the present case book, thus, has the ambitious goal of helping to provide students with a working knowledge of statistics — of both tools for thinking about business problems and of using the computer for applying that knowledge to solve everyday business problems. We will put students "behind the desk" in a life-like business setting, present them with "real-world" issues, and give them a chance to put their understanding to work.

CASES

We have chosen a number of specific "data-relevant" business issues around which to develop computer-based cases. They were chosen with three goals in mind.

1. We have chosen case topics to reflect a wide range of scenarios over several functional business areas — management, marketing, advertising, production and operations management, human resource strategy and the like. While written to reflect a wide range of functional business areas, we have attempted to write cases that do not require a great deal of prior functional expertise in those areas. More importantly, we have attempted to choose topics that typify the real-world problems that are faced by real-world managers

all the time — correctly interpreting data, choosing between costly alternatives, determining the quantity and price of goods to go into a business proposal, choosing a new strategy from data that reflect both positive and negative consequences, and so forth. We wanted to represent the kind of issues, problems and decisions that students can be expected to be involved with — business problems that require people to use good judgment and make a good decision.

2. We wanted to insure that the cases, as a set, sample a broad range of statistical procedures. Most of these statistical procedures should be covered in entry-level business statistics classes. Instructors should have no trouble identifying cases that match the specific topic coverage of their course using the cross-tabulation of cases with statistical methods included in the Instructor's Guide. Students will note that data from several of these cases can be analyzed using more than one statistical procedure — for example, one could analyze some data sets using analysis of variance or by using regression analysis. In all such instances, even though the analysis might be different, be assured that the "correct decision" is the same!

3. We wanted to emphasize that many business decisions do not require a Ph. D. in statistics in order to arrive at a good business solution. Many times, all that's needed is for someone to "statistically summarize" the data in a simple, meaningful manner. Thus, you'll see several cases that are focused specifically on descriptive summarizations of data sets, portraying those statistical summaries graphically (*e.g.*, using histograms or boxplots), and accurately interpreting these results and displays. It is our belief that many of the "data-relevant" problems students will face in the business world will require little more than a strong background in descriptive statistics. Helping students be good at what's most commonly required seems like a good investment in their development! In other instances, where a more advanced statistical understanding is required, basic statistical summaries and graphs are still very useful and will help students make sense of the results of more complex statistical analyses.

COMPUTER REQUIREMENTS

Students can expect their instructor to choose cases that reflect the material being covered in class and in their text book. Most college business statistics courses require students to use a microcomputer or mainframe statistical software package — clearly that will be true if this case book is assigned. Instructors will provide needed help in using that software package. In the event that a mainframe computer package is used, it may be desirable for the instructor to upload a copy of the data files to the mainframe for easier student access. Likewise, in a networked micro-computer environment, it may be advantageous to make a copy of the data files available on the network.

The data files on the Data Disk for this case book were designed specifically to work with most popular business statistical software packages. (These cases could also be analyzed with a spreadsheet package such as Excel which has some statistical capabilities.) Each data set includes only numerical data, in ASCII (text) format. Students who en-counter any problems with reading the data into their software package should see their instructor. We have tried the data files with a number of popular statistics packages (including Minitab, Systat, and Execustat) and have noted any limitations, as well as problems and their solutions, in the Instructor's Guide.

A complete description of each data set is given in the Data Description section of each case. Names and definitions for each variable (*i.e.*, for each column of data) are provided.

Finally, in some instances, cases require students to prepare graphs and/or tables describing the results. If the chosen statistical software enables students to do so, they should use it. Otherwise, students can summarize the data statistically using their statistical software and then prepare graphs and/or tables by hand or use any of the common graphics packages (*e.g.*, Harvard Graphics) that may be available to students.

IN CONCLUSION, . . .

We believe that both students and instructors will find these business statistics cases to be an interesting and valuable addition to their business statistics course. Our experiences with this approach have been extremely rewarding. We hope yours are, too.

Amtech, Inc.

Amtech, Inc. is in the business of selling sophisticated computerized point-of-sale cash registers, cash register printers, computer-printer software and interfaces, printer supplies, and hands-on training to commercial accounts. Amtech's owners chose their market niche to be smaller companies that appear ready for a large scale expansion of their business. Smaller companies need, and are willing to pay for, the personal attention and customization of the hardware, software and training that Amtech offers. Once committed to a particular configuration of hardware and software, these clients seldom reconsider their alternatives when expansion occurs. This is a high margin business and no client is considered too small to deserve attention. Small clients often blossom into larger businesses, and their growth typically signals the expansion of Amtech's sales as well.

The typical marketing plan is centered on identifying customer needs and then developing a plan to satisfy those needs. Amtech's first contact with potential clients demonstrates their cash registers' capabilities and the extent to which software can be customized to meet a particular client's needs. Amtech account executives emphasize the importance of customizing both their software and training to meet clients' needs as the features that distinguish Amtech from its competitors. They then request an opportunity to distribute a questionnaire to key personnel in the client organization in order to develop a customization plan that "fits" the client's needs and to make a presentation to the client based on their findings.

The questionnaire asks participants about important business issues needed to customize the software, and the backgrounds of those persons who will use the high tech equipment in order to customize the training program. Part I of the questionnaire deals with technical business issues that reflect the nature of the client's business and business plan. For example, information is collected regarding their accounting system, the inventory monitoring, control and reordering functions, the extent to which the client wishes to create a data base of client purchases as a marketing tool, and the selection and printing of in-store coupons on the back of the sales receipt designed to elicit future purchases that complement current purchases. These business functions, among others, are discussed with the management of the organization and go into designing the software to meet client's business needs. All senior level management and headquarters' professional staff (*e.g.*, accountants) complete this part of the questionnaire.

The second part of the questionnaire is aimed at understanding the backgrounds of those persons who will use the equipment. This is important information, since the training program will have to be designed to meet the needs of those persons who will complete the questionnaire. If the typical employee has limited background in the use of computers, then a longer, more costly training program will need to be designed. On the other hand, if their background with computers is substantial, then a mere orientation to the use of this equipment might suffice. This is an important consideration from more than the training costs involved, since a great deal of evidence that exists suggests that poorly trained employees either become frustrated and quit, or if they stay, never help the company reap the full benefit of the technology it has purchased.

Wendy Cambridge began her career at Amtech less than two years ago and has risen quickly from marketing assistant to assistant account manager for some of Amtech's larger clients. She was recently given her first opportunity to co-lead a sales team for a new potential client, Grass-Roots, Inc.

Grass-Roots fits the profile of an ideal customer. They are setting up a small chain of plant and garden stores in a large Southern city and have plans to expand their company to ten additional cities over the next five years. Each store location will be surveyed to insure high levels of customer service. Operations staff will work individually with customers, from when they first walk in the store through check-out.

The Amtech sales team has made their initial presentation to Grass-Roots, who have agreed to allow Amtech to do a follow-up survey to see exactly how Amtech can help them. Amtech knows they have their "foot in the door" and can make a potentially lucrative sale depending on how good a job the sales team does from this point on.

Wendy Cambridge was put in charge of administering the questionnaire and preparing a presentation on Grass-Roots' training needs. This is her first time to head any part of a sales effort and she wants to do it well. While she has never interpreted survey results, written a proposal or made a sales presentation on her own, she has worked directly for Mary Gordon, Amtech's Corporate Sales Manager, on these assignments and feels confident in her ability to take on these responsibilities.

Wendy administered the Amtech questionnaire to all current management and operations employees in their headquarters and three retail store locations. In total, she met with and distributed the questionnaire to all six corporate management and professional staff and, in the stores, to a total of nine management and 33 operations staff. Each store employs a manager and two assistant managers, plus an operations staff of 11 persons. She asked only headquarters' managers and professional staff to complete Part I of the questionnaire; everybody was asked to complete Part II. All employees completed the questionnaire on company time, in small group settings. Wendy prepared a computerized file containing the survey data and then analyzed the data regarding employee background using a common PC statistical software package.

Wendy then examined the results from Part II of this questionnaire administration, and based on her analyses, developed a training proposal. In preparation for her presentation to Grass-Roots, she also prepared charts (shown below) that summarized her findings.

Survey Results for Grass-Roots Employees

	Responses	Mean	Std. Dev.
Age	48	29.5	10.4
Computer Knowledge	27	3.0	1.3

Race

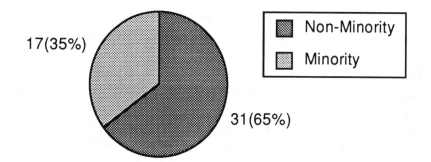

17(35%)

31(65%)

Non-Minority
Minority

Sex

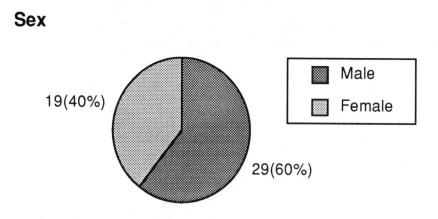

19(40%)

29(60%)

Male
Female

Education Level

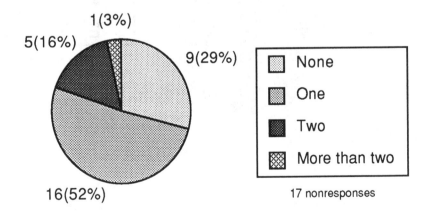

5(13%) 1(3%)

9(23%)

16(40%)

9(23%)

Less than HS

HS Diploma

Some College

College Degree

Graduate Work

8 nonresponses

Computer Courses

1(3%)

5(16%)

9(29%)

16(52%)

None

One

Two

More than two

17 nonresponses

Used a Computer?

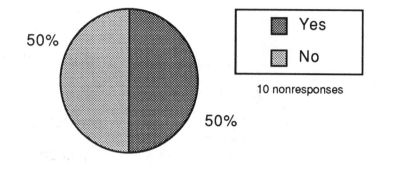

50%

50%

Yes
No

10 nonresponses

Own a Computer?

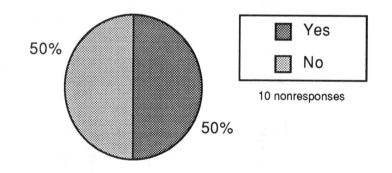

50%

50%

Yes
No

10 nonresponses

Self-Rated Computer Knowledge

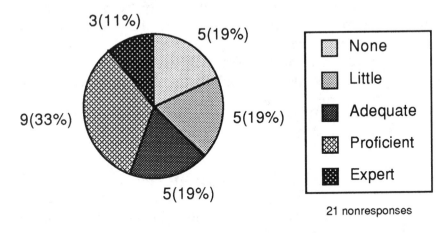

3(11%) 5(19%)

9(33%) 5(19%)

5(19%)

Legend:
- None
- Little
- Adequate
- Proficient
- Expert

21 nonresponses

    In brief form, Wendy suggested that employees of Grass-Roots were reasonably computer literate and, as a result, would need only minimal training — possibly little more than an orientation program, a brief tutorial on the use of the cash registers, and a question and answer session. She based her conclusion on survey results that she interpreted as follows:

(1) Employees have a relatively high level of education.

(2) More than half of the employees have taken at least one computer course.

(3) More than half of the employees use or have used a computer on their present or prior jobs.

(4) Half of the employees own a PC.

(5) The average level of self-rated computer sophistication is at the adequate level of understanding.

While Wendy's background is not in business, she has a track record of doing good work and of growing as her responsibilities are increased. Like most people, however, Wendy makes mistakes in her early efforts on new projects. When given feedback, she quickly "catches on" and can be counted on to learn from her lessons well. For this reason, Mary Gordon has decided to give Wendy some backup help to insure that she has the necessary "safety net" on her new assignment. Mary thinks a lot of Wendy's potential and knows that a little help early in her career will help make her a successful contributor for years to come.

Assignment

You have been assigned to be Wendy's "safety net." Look over the survey results and judge whether or not Wendy has correctly analyzed and interpreted the results from this survey. You'll find the data in AMTECH.DAT on the Data Disk. A description of this data set is provided in the Data Description section. Prepare a brief report for Mary Gordon that reflects your interpretation of the survey's results, and that makes a recommendation regarding your support for Wendy's training proposal. Finally, prepare a chart that reflects the computer literacy of relevant Grass-Roots personnel. The Case Questions will assist you in your analysis of the data. Use important details from your analysis to support your recommendations.

Data Description

File AMTECH.DAT on the Data Disk contains the coded data from the survey of Grass-Roots employees. Data are recorded in the manner depicted below. A "*" indicates non-response or missing information. (See the Important Note below.)

ID	JOB	RACE	AGE	SEX	ED	COURSES	USED	OWN	KNOW
1	3	2	24	1	3	1	2	2	2
2	1	1	42	2	5	1	2	2	4
3	3	2	19	1	*	*	*	*	*
4	3	1	22	2	2	*	1	1	*
⋮	⋮	⋮	⋮	⋮	⋮	⋮	⋮	⋮	⋮

The variables are defined as follows:

ID: Survey identification number.

JOB: 1 = Headquarters Management and Professional Staff,
2 = Store Management,
3 = Store Operations Staff.

RACE: 1 = non-minority,
2 = minority.

AGE: Age on last birthday.

SEX: 1 = female,
2 = male.

ED: 1 = less than a high school diploma,
2 = high school diploma,
3 = some college work,
4 = college degree,
5 = graduate work or degree.

COURSES: Number of computer courses taken.

USED: Has the employee used a computer?
          0 = no,
          1 = yes.

OWN: Does the employee own a computer?
          0 = no,
          1 = yes.

KNOW: Self-evaluation of computer knowledge using a rating
          scale, where
          1 = no knowledge,
          2 = little knowledge,
          3 = adequate knowledge,
          4 = better than adequate knowledge,
          5 = expert level of knowledge.

IMPORTANT NOTE: The symbol "*" (asterisk) is used in the data file AMTECH.DAT to denote non-response or missing data. Consult your statistical software documentation for a list of valid missing data codes. If your statistical software package does not accept "*" as a valid missing code, you have two options. Your statistical software package may allow you to specify another missing code. Otherwise, you will need to change each occurrence of "*" in the data file to a missing symbol that is acceptable to your particular statistics package. This can be done by editing the file AMTECH.DAT within a word processing package. See your instructor if you need assistance.

Case Questions: Amtech, Inc.

Name _____

1. Was Wendy Cambridge's interpretation of the survey results flawed? Explain.

2. Describe the "computer literacy" of those employees who will use the new point-of-sale cash registers. Be sure to describe (a) the sample of employees on which you based your interpretation and (b) the statistical results of your analyses.

3. Based on your analyses, what is your recommendation regarding needed training for Grass-Roots employees?

4. Explain the business implications of your recommendation versus that of Wendy Cambridge.

5. Prepare a chart, in graphic or tabular form, that summarizes the results from your analyses of the survey data and that can be used to make key points in the sales presentation. Attach your chart to this assignment.

Plastiks, Inc.

Plastiks is a moderately sized manufacturing company that specializes in making unusual, custom parts, subassemblies, and fasteners from malleable synthetic materials. When client companies have a need for a non-standard component in the assembly of one of their products, they often turn to companies like Plastiks who specialize in designing and manufacturing the needed components. The professional staff at Plastiks are the Customer Representatives who work directly with client companies to design these innovative, customized "solutions" to customers' manufacturing problems. They work closely with clients to insure that the part, subassembly, or fastener they design actually solves the clients' manufacturing problem.

The technical staff picks up where the professional staff leaves off. Their job, entitled Design Engineer, is to figure out how to make the innovative solutions at the quality level demanded by the customer in a time frame and at a cost that meets their customers' needs. Design Engineers work only within their technical specialty area. They have the responsibility of not only engineering the component to insure it meets client needs, but also to design a production process that makes the manufacture of that product feasible, quick, and affordable. Design Engineers then work closely with manufacturing to insure that product design gets accurately translated into high quality products. Their work is not done until the final product leaves the shipping docks for their customers' facility.

Not surprisingly, Plastiks has developed an excellent reputation in the specialty manufacturing business. As this reputation began to grow, so did

Plastiks. From a company of just over 65 people in 1962, Plastiks now employs nearly 150 persons in their two plant locations. They have grown from a two-division company specializing in Plastic and Resin processes to a four-division company specializing in two additional advanced processes (Polymers and Poly-Carbon Compounds) by 1985. Their organization structure has correspondingly evolved into specialized processes that require expertise in one of these particular advanced technologies. As the need for more varied technical expertise grew, Plastiks hired graduates from doctoral programs at some of this nation's finest universities to fill Design Engineer positions.

Recently, Don Betsill attended an executive development seminar that discussed the importance of strategic planning. The seminar's main theme was that the business environment was so complex and so dynamic that one should not assume that past practices would continue to be effective into the future. Rather, the seminar suggested that CEO's conduct "strategic long-range planning" activities to insure that their companies were capable of meeting the new business challenges they would face down the road.

Don Betsill took this message to heart. Upon returning to Plastiks, he hired a consultant to assist him in his long-range planning efforts. The consultant, Jennifer Shipp, explained the several different components of her planning program.

According to the consultant, strategic long-range planning begins with a careful self-study of the company's current conditions. Shipp said the company should begin by forming a number of committees to do a series of analyses that would result in a clear understanding of the company's external threats and opportunities and its internal strengths and weaknesses. Each committee would make a report to Plastiks' executive committee at a planning conference, at which time future plans would be discussed. Betsill formed a number of committees to focus on each of these important areas.

One committee, headed by Peggy Koehler, was formed to examine the "health" of the company's key positions — those jobs necessary for the company to be successful now and in five to seven years down the road. Koehler's committee wasted little time in identifying the Design Engineer and Customer Representative positions as keys to both the near term and long term success of the company.

Her committee then spent an hour discussing what needed to be done to "study" these key positions, but the answer wasn't clear. As a result, Peggy Koehler asked the consultant to attend their next committee meeting to discuss how to proceed with this assignment. At that meeting, Jennifer Shipp told the committee, "I'm an expert in planning. Your committee has to be the experts in the plastics manufacturing business. Ask yourselves, what's important about those positions? Are they easy to do? How often does someone quit? How easy is it to replace someone? Must you go to the outside for replacements, or can you develop people inside the company for these positions as they come open? If the latter is true, do you have such people waiting in the wings, or will there be a crisis if you suddenly lose a key person? You might also want to insure that the company isn't vulnerable to legal liabilities under Federal fair employment laws — you know, that you're protected against charges of discrimination."

With this advice in hand, Koehler and her committee set out to gather information about these key positions. They collected a great deal of information on each function. They easily concluded that (1) their business depended on these key jobs being performed effectively, (2) it takes a great deal of time for persons to develop expertise in these areas, and (3) it would be difficult to find people in the job market to replace key persons, if openings were to occur.

They then set out to collect descriptive information about the incumbents in these key jobs. Data were collected on age, race, gender, job tenure, and job performance. It was at this point that Koehler and her committee started to again have questions about how to proceed. In a conversation with Jennifer Shipp, Peggy Koehler asked, "Now that we've collected descriptive information about people in these two key areas, what exactly do we do?" Jennifer Shipp responded, "There is no simple formula here. You need to use your judgment — your managerial judgment. If you were CEO and saw these data, would you be concerned? Look back at the issues I spoke about at our earlier meeting and ask yourself whether these two functions were adequately staffed, whether job losses are imminent, where replacements would come from and the legal implications of Plastiks' hiring patterns. Then, as I said, use your judgment. Are you happy or bothered with what you see? If you're bothered, explain why and be prepared to defend your position. That's all there is to it."

Peggy Koehler and her committee felt somewhat better with the guidance they just received, but still weren't sure about exactly what they were supposed to do. But, since the planning conference meeting wasn't very far down the road, they proceeded with their task and finished two weeks before the scheduled planning conference.

Peggy Koehler was nervous enough about what she and her committee had done that she asked Jennifer Shipp if she would listen to a "dry run" of her presentation. Jennifer agreed. The next day, Peggy presented her committee's findings to Jennifer Shipp. She prepared a series of statistical graphs (shown below) depicting the key results from her committee's analysis and made four points based on them. She began, "After analyzing, discussing, and interpreting the results of our analyses, we concluded that, with one exception, the company is in "good health" regarding its two key positions — Design Engineering and Customer Representatives. I'll explain our conclusion by making four points."

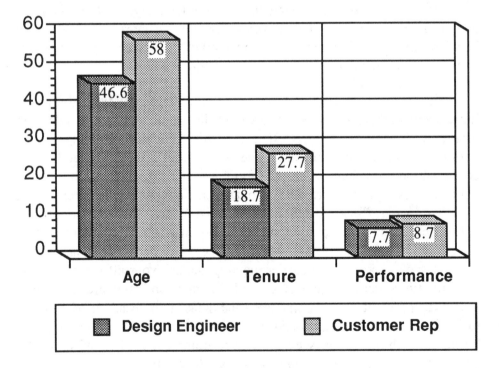

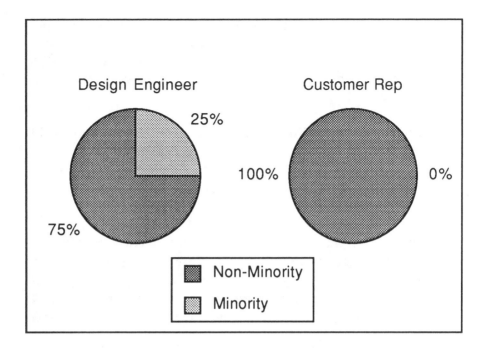

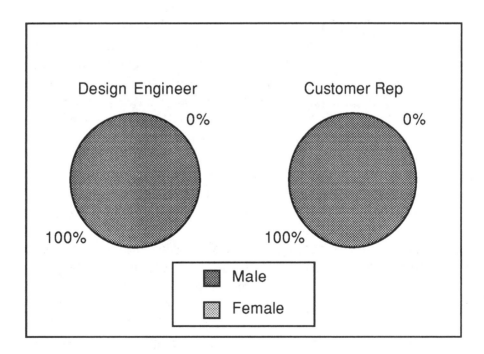

1. The performance ratings of persons on the Design Engineer and Customer Representative jobs are excellent. On the company's nine-point rating scale, the ratings range from just under an 8 for the Design Engineer job and just under a perfect 9 on the Customer Representative job.

2. Such excellent performance is to be expected given the solid base of experience on these jobs. Average tenure ranges from approximately 19 years in the Design Engineering area to nearly 28 years on the Customer Rep job.

3. Not surprisingly, our Professional and Technical staffs tend to be older, averaging from the mid-40's to the late-50's in age. We do want to note a problem here regarding age in the Customer Rep job — given that the average age suggests that our Customer Reps are approaching retirement age, we might want to be alert to identifying their replacements over the next five to seven years.

4. At first we were somewhat surprised with the distribution of race and gender — we appear to be predominantly white and male in these key positions, especially in the Customer Rep job. This apparent problem is, however, easily explained by the number of years of experience these staff members have. This, again, is particularly true on the Customer Rep job. Plastiks was not sensitive to the issues associated with hiring minorities and women 20 or 30 years ago, when most of these employees were hired. Over the past ten years, however, Plastiks has taken this issue more seriously and, as a result, has made great strides in becoming more "affirmative" in their hiring practices. We, therefore, feel this problem will rectify itself over time.

Jennifer Shipp listened attentively to these conclusions, and noted that Peggy seemed very uneasy. She asked Peggy if the members of her committee were "comfortable" with their conclusions. Peggy confessed that they were not and asked again for Jennifer's help with this project. Peggy noted, "None of us have ever worked on a project like this before. We'd be most grateful for any help you might provide." Jennifer said she would talk with Mr. Betsill and see what might be done.

The next day, Jennifer Shipp called Peggy Koehler to tell her that "help was on the way." Don Betsill acknowledged that this task might be confusing for persons who had never had the opportunity to "think from data" and, given that it was such an important part of the planning process, he agreed to provide help. He assigned some additional people to her committee to take another look at the data and reach their own conclusions regarding what the data meant. They would report their results directly to Peggy Koehler and, in essence, indicate whether or not they agreed with the committee's conclusions, and if not, would indicate how they differed.

Assignment

You have been assigned to the group of persons who will help Peggy Koehler with her assignment. Look at the data, provided in the PLASTIKS.DAT file on the Data Disk and described in the Data Description section. Examine this information and attempt to determine if Plastiks, Inc. has reason to be concerned about their key jobs. If you believe that Peggy Koehler's conclusions and transparencies are inaccurate, prepare a new set to summarize your analyses and thinking. Then, prepare a brief report summarizing your conclusions for Peggy Koehler. The Case Questions will guide your thinking on this assignment. Use important details from your analysis to support your recommendation.

Data Description

The PLASTIKS.DAT file contains data describing employees on the Design Engineering, Assistant Customer Representative and Customer Representative jobs. A partial listing of the data is shown below.

Job Type	Job	Age	Race	Gender	Tenure	Performance
1	1	59	1	1	32	9
1	1	62	1	1	33	9
1	1	61	1	1	32	9
1	2	60	1	1	31	9
1	2	58	1	1	30	9
⋮	⋮	⋮	⋮	⋮	⋮	⋮

These data are coded as follows:

Job Type
: 1, if technical position,
2, if professional staff position.

Job:
: Specific job assignment (1 = plastics, 2 = resins, 3 = polymers, 4 = poly-carbon, and 5 = customer representative).

Age:
: Age of job incumbent, in years.

Race:
: 1, if non-minority,
0, if minority.

Gender:
: 1, if male,
0, if female.

Tenure:
: Years of experience on the job.

Performance:
: Most recent job performance rating on the company's 9-point rating scale where 1 = poor performance and 9 = excellent performance.

Case Questions: Plastiks, Inc.

Name _____

1. How many different Design Engineer specialties are there?

2. What are the average performance, tenure, and age of people in each of the four specific Design Engineer jobs?

3. What percentage of employees on these specific jobs are minorities? What percentage are females?

4. How soon can one expect persons on each of these five jobs to retire? Does this suggest a problem for Plastiks to handle? Explain.

5. Are there any performance problems indicated in your analysis of the data? Does this suggest a problem for Plastiks to handle? Explain.

6. What evidence in the data supports Peggy Koehler's suggestion that Plastiks is becoming more "affirmative" in their hiring practices?

7. Do you agree with Peggy Koehler's conclusion that "with one exception, the company was in 'good health' regarding its key positions?" Explain.

The Keels Agency

The Keels Agency (TKA) is a small advertising agency in Portland, Oregon that helps clients get the biggest return on their advertising dollars. TKA specializes in working with companies that are looking to advertise their products and services for the first time. Such companies are typically newer businesses that have begun to grow and now have the revenues to take the next step by investing in advertising. TKA has a good track record of helping these companies feel comfortable with their expenditure of advertising dollars. As pointed out by Beth Keels, founder and CEO of this agency, the costs incurred with advertising can be considerable and are always perceived as a relatively high percentage of clients' revenues. For first-time clients, the thought of investing in advertising, no matter how much sense it might make, always leads to questions about whether the expense will be worth the investment.

Companies like TKA typically try to identify the particular market segments that are most likely to buy their clients goods and services and then locate an advertising outlet that will reach this particular market group. Client groups require considerable explanation about how this "matching" occurs. Beth Keels typically explains it like this:

> We collect a lot of information on clients' actual sales over a two to three month period and on the people who make those purchases. We get this information from a variety of sources, including surveys, interviews, credit records, mailing lists, contests, and so forth. Our goal is to learn as much as we can about our clients' customers to see whether there might be a distinct "profile" of the typical customer for a particular product or service. If a distinct

profile emerges from our research, then we try to match that profile to advertising outlets, such as TV, radio, newspapers, and magazines known to be watched, listened to or read by people with this particular profile. In this way, we target advertising directly to high potential customers. This procedure goes a long way in helping our clients feel more comfortable that at least the money spent on advertising is putting their products and services in front of the right audience. We've been doing it this way for years and have a long track record of being successful.

TKA recently signed a new client, Cycle World, in nearby Seattle. Cycle World markets, under its own name, three lines of racing and mountain bikes, made by several bicycle manufacturers. Cycle World currently sells its bikes in their six retail outlets in major cities throughout the Northwest. Cycle World is now ready to launch a direct sales campaign of their products by advertising bicycles in nationally-distributed magazines.

This direct sales effort will rely on reaching potential customers by placing half-page, two-color ads in popular magazines that have large, national subscription bases. The marketing campaign would attempt to (1) create name recognition for Cycle World's products based on placing five ads in each issue of chosen magazines, and (2) offer customers savings that result from eliminating the "middle-man." Thus, it is clear that choosing target magazines for each product is crucial in order to insure that Cycle World's new venture will be successful. They have set aside $240,000 to advertise their products in this manner. In addition to the costs of placing the ads, this budget must also cover TKA's separate charges to Cycle World for the creation and production of the advertising copy as well as their fee and overhead charges. Choosing the wrong magazine not only means that this total budget is being spent on multiple ads to reach the wrong audience, but that the real potential customers would still go unreached.

Cycle World sells three lines of bicycles. The lower line includes "basic" racing and mountain bikes. These bicycles, made by the largest bicycle manufacturer in the U. S., tend to be heavy as far as bikes go, have relatively few features and offer few customer options. Their middle line, made by a popular West Coast manufacturer, includes bicycles that are made of light-weight metals, have many features that serious bikers want and that provide a modest number of options to help buyers customize their bikes. The upper line is made by one of Europe's leading bicycle manufacturers, and includes bicycles that are made of ultra-light alloy metals, that have all the "bells and whistles" which can be put on a bike. Customers are allowed to choose among a number of options to customize their purchases from the upper line of bicycles.

Beth Keels put together a market research team to identify the profile of the typical customer for each product line. To collect this information, the market research team collected information from persons who purchased bicycles at Cycle World's six retail stores. A random sample of customers during a two-month period was asked to complete a short survey that contained descriptive questions about themselves. To encourage customers to complete the survey, each was offered as a gift for their participation, a biker's helmet, a mileage meter, or a bicycle tire pump. Over 90 percent of the sampled customers completed the survey. Questions were chosen to get an understanding of the demographic background (*i.e.*, age, gender, marital status, education) and the interest level in biking (*i.e.*, extent of use, fitness level, and self-rated interest) of customers.

Based on these data, a profile of the "typical" customer for each product line of merchandise needed to be created and compared to the "typical" subscriber profile for a list of magazines. The list of potential magazines was chosen to reflect three issues: (a) the subscriber base needed to be a national one, (b) the subscriber list needed to fall in the moderate size category for nationally-distributed magazines, and (c) the magazine needed to focus on a particular topic or theme.

Cycle World very specifically wanted to reach a national market in their first attempt to enter the direct sales arena. They reasoned that this was the best way to guard against the problems created by unpredictable, cyclical, regional economic downturns. The choice of looking at magazines in the moderate-sized national subscription base would mean that ads would be similar in costs and within Cycle World's advertising budget. Finally, the typical subscriber was expected to represent a larger proportion of the subscriber base for magazines with a particular focus or theme. The list of potential magazine outlets, and the profile of the typical customer for each, are provided in Table 1. The magazines in Table 1 were chosen as possible advertising outlets because they have a moderately large national subscription base and focus on particular themes.

Table 1. Potential Advertising Outlets for Cycle World

Magazines	Age	% Male	Education	Salary	Level
ALIVE!	26	45	BA	26,000	5
Business World	30	70	BA	50,000	4
Chinese Cooking	38	30	HS/BA	34,000	3
Computer Technician	34	92	Tech/BA	37,000	2
Country Cookin'	32	20	HS	20,000	2
Crafters	32	30	HS/BA	34,000	3
Creative Projects	28	20	HS/BA	32,000	4
Cycle Time	29	65	BA	60,000	5
Electronics Today	42	90	Tech/BA	42,000	2
Entrepreneur's Day	26	90	HS	27,000	3
Family Living	30	55	HS/BA	31,000	3
Fashion Flair	20	10	HS	14,000	4
Fisherman's Line	50	90	HS	34,000	3
Gourmet's Kitchen	46	60	BA	56,000	3
Outdoor Fun	27	55	HS/BA	30,000	3
Naturalists	38	60	BA	45,000	3
Parent's Digest	28	50	HS/BA	29,000	2
Runners' World	43	70	BA	38,000	5
RV Country	57	69	HS/BA	28,000	2
Software Review	28	60	BA	48,000	4
Sporting World	28	52	HS/BA	31,000	4
Sports Line	35	76	HS	28,000	4
Today's Cyclist	25	10	HS	22,000	2
Today's Home Video	32	40	BA	36,000	2
Traveler's Digest	46	60	HS/BA	44,000	4
Who's Hot In The Movies	29	45	HS/BA	29,000	2
Who's Hot In Music	22	30	HS	18,000	3
Who's Hot In Sports	25	80	HS	22,000	3
Woman's World Today	28	10	BA	34,000	3
Wood Crafters	42	85	HS/BA	42,000	3

The data in Table 1 reflect the average age, salary, activity level of subscribers (1 = none to 5 = very active), the percent of subscribers who are male, and the modal educational background of subscribers (HS = high school diploma, BA = bachelor's degree, and Tech = technical certificate from a trade school). The average cost of a half-page ad in these magazines is approximately $2,000 per issue.

Assignment

As a member of the market research team, your job is to examine the data that contains descriptive information about Cycle World's customers. You'll find the data in KEELS.DAT on the Data Disk. A description of this data set is provided in the Data Description section.

You will need to analyze these data in order to create a profile of the "typical" customer for each line of merchandise. Once done, compare your understanding of the typical customer for each product line to the "typical" subscribers given in Table 1. Based on this comparison, make recommendations about which magazines should be targeted as advertising outlets for each product line. Finally, estimate that the total cost for advertising all products. Assume that each ad will take a half-page and run five times in each issue and in four issues a year. The Case Questions will assist you in your analysis of the data. Use important details from your analysis to support your recommendation.

Data Description

File KEELS.DAT on the Data Disk contains the coded data from the survey of Cycle World customers. Data are recorded in the manner depicted below.

Product Line	Age	Sex	Education	Marital Status	Income	Times/ Week	Miles/ Week	Fitness
3	22	1	4	1	26000	3	120	5
2	50	1	4	2	41000	2	60	3
1	50	2	4	2	47000	3	70	3
2	19	1	3	1	18000	3	60	2
3	48	1	4	1	26000	3	120	5
⋮	⋮	⋮	⋮	⋮	⋮	⋮	⋮	⋮

These data are coded as follows:

Product Line: 1 = low product line,
2 = middle product line,
3 = high product line.

Age: Age on last birthday.

Sex: 1 = male,
2 = female.

Education: 1 = no high school diploma,
2 = high school diploma,
3 = some college-level work,
4 = college degree,
5 = graduate work or degree.

Marital Status: 1 = single,
2 = married.

Income: Annual family income, rounded off to the nearest $1000.

Times/Week:	Average number of times the person uses or plans to use bicycle each week.
Miles/Week:	Average number of miles completed or planned each week.
Fitness:	Self-rated fitness level, based on scale ranging from 1 = poor shape to 5 = excellent shape.

Case Questions: The Keels Agency

Name _____

1. Describe the profile of the "typical" customer for each product line. Be sure you use statistical indices that are appropriate for the data being analyzed.

2. Compare each of these product-line profiles to the profiles of typical subscribers of the magazines listed in Table 1. Recommend the two most appropriate magazine outlets for advertising each separate product line.

3. Based on matching product-line and subscriber profiles, how many <u>different</u> magazine outlets are needed to insure that each product line is advertised <u>twice</u>? List the final set of magazine outlets that you recommend.

4. Estimate the total cost of advertising bicycles in the chosen magazines. Assume that each half-page ad will run five times in each issue and in four issues a year.

5. What percent of the total advertising budget does your recommendation represent?

Glenco Bonus Program

Everybody at Glenco, a moderate-sized manufacturing company, is talking about the new incentive bonus program. Last August, John Marchant, CEO of Glenco, announced a new program designed to encourage the best efforts of persons on the production floor. While production employees could count on regular pay raises as usual, Glenco would now be offering a $500 bonus to the top 20 percent of all production workers. Thus, of the 155 employees, 31 (or so) persons could expect to get a nice surprise just in time for Christmas.

The reaction to Marchant's announcement was immediate, and mixed. Clearly, there were a number of employees who liked the new bonus plan. In fact, a few persons laid bets on being among the top 20 percent. Sam Miller, Pete Cravens, Mike Sanders and Tom Reeves decided to pool their bonuses on a new fishing boat that the four of them would share, and they actually made a down payment on it in early November. Even Harvey Fried, who seldom spoke out about anything, was overheard telling some of his friends about "... how nice it will be to finally get some recognition for all my good work around here."

Not all the talk, however, was positive. There were, of course, those persons who knew that they would never receive a bonus. They complained loudly and often about the proposed bonus plan and suggested any number of "better" uses for the money. For example, Frank Phillips thought that the money was better spent on underwriting dental insurance for everybody and Martha Renner thought the money would be better spent on day care benefits. Other employees had still other suggestions for use of the money.

Even management reaction was split. The most vocal negative reaction came from Mark Brown, one of the more senior foremen at Glenco. Mark said that he had seen incentive programs like this before on three previous jobs. He said that they never seemed to be fairly administered and, as a result, always caused more problems than they seemed to solve. Mark said, "Programs like this never seem to work out smoothly. When people who expect the bonus don't get it, they just get angry and make life unpleasant for the rest of us. I wish we had never opened this can of worms!"

In spite of the complaints, plans for implementing the new bonus plan were made. A new committee, named the Employee Bonus Committee, was formed to choose the bonus recipients. This committee was comprised of five manufacturing managers. They were to make their choices based on supervisory ratings of employee performance. This was the normal way of evaluating employees' performance.

Supervisors normally made their ratings in late November, using Glenco's standard performance appraisal form. Prior use of this form to assess performance has resulted in reasonably satisfactory results, although it appearred that some supervisors ignore the company's request to keep their average ratings near the scale midpoint on the 10-point rating scale (1 = poor performance, 10 = excellent performance). Even training did not seem to help equate supervisors on the standards they used to evaluate their subordinates. For the most part, however, this did not seem to cause any problems, since performance had not been used as the basis for making salary adjustments or for distributing other types of rewards to manufacturing employees in the past. In fact, evaluations served little more than to formally document poor performance for employees who were put on notice to improve their work or face a pink slip!

This year, the ratings were to be turned in directly to the Employee Bonus Committee. Their job would be to choose the employees who had earned the bonus and to explain how they were chosen (*i.e.*, be prepared to defend their choices to disgruntled employees who did not receive the bonus).

Assignment

The chairman of the EBC, Tom Marlin, has asked each member of the committee to come to the first meeting with a list of "winners." You are a member of this committee. Use the data contained in the file GLENCO.DAT on the Data Disk. This file contains information on ID number, gender, race, age, department number and performance rating for each employee. Analyze these data and make your list of employees whom you believe are deserving of the $500 bonus (the list should include approximately 20% of the employees). Describe the statistical procedures you used to come up with this list, and explain why your procedures will result in the fair treatment of all employees at Glenco (*i.e.*, defend your reasoning for making those choices at the EBC meeting). (Hint: You might want to look at, and compare, the distributions of ratings given by the supervisors.)

Data Description

The data for the Glenco Manufacturing case are contained in the file GLENCO.DAT on the Data Disk. The file contains information on 155 employees. In addition to their ID number, the data file includes information on sex, race, and age for all employees as well as their department number and performance rating. A complete listing of the data on the disk is shown below. **Note, however, that the names of the employees are not included in the disk file GLENCO.DAT.** The alphabetical listing of Glenco employees given here can be used to find the names corresponding to the employee ID numbers in answering Case Question #1.

In the file GLENCO.DAT, the variables are defined as follows:

ID: Employee identification number.

Sex: 1, if female,
          2, if male.

Race: 1, if minority,
          2, if non-minority.

Age: Age in years.

Dept: Department number (1-7).

Rating: Employee performance rating (1-10) as given by the departmental supervisor, with 10 as the highest rating and 1 as the lowest rating.

Alphabetical Listing of Glenco Employees

Last Name	First Name	ID	Sex	Race	Age	Dept	Rating
Alexander	Charles	001	2	2	35	1	5
Ammann	Ray	002	2	2	60	1	5
Anderson	James	003	2	1	61	2	4
Babcock	Marilyn	004	1	1	36	2	5
Bagley	Jan	005	1	2	40	5	8
Baker	Lisa	006	1	2	59	3	6
Baldwin	Lois	007	1	1	35	4	5
Bartlett	Bill	008	2	1	26	4	4
Blair	Elizabeth	009	1	2	41	6	5
Bolden	Holly	010	1	2	50	6	4
Bowling	Frances	011	1	2	22	7	8
Brown	Charlotte	012	1	2	62	7	4
Bruton	Penny	013	1	2	23	7	4
Campbell	Delores	014	1	1	43	7	5
Cash	Bill	015	2	1	35	7	7
Chandler	Margo	016	1	2	42	4	7
Chang	Sally	017	1	2	25	4	6
Clark	John	018	2	2	29	5	7
Cook	Debbie	019	1	2	43	2	6
Cravens	Pete	020	2	1	55	5	8
Crowder	Thomas	021	2	1	20	2	5
Cummings	Jeanette	022	1	2	43	1	6
Cunningham	Sherry	023	1	2	48	3	8
Davis	Ruth	024	1	1	44	2	5
Dawson	Michael	025	2	2	24	2	5
Dickens	Jimmy	026	2	2	60	5	7
Dorsey	Patricia	027	1	2	44	3	8
Drake	Annette	028	1	2	20	7	5
Echols	Betty	029	1	2	41	7	5
Ellis	Betty	030	1	1	55	6	5

England	David	031	2	2	30	6	7
Ennis	Jerry	032	2	2	27	1	5
Ernst	Faye	033	1	2	43	3	6
Esterline	Laura	034	1	2	39	5	8
Ferguson	Sylvia	035	1	2	31	5	8
Fields	Anne	036	1	2	46	1	5
Flores	Bo	037	2	2	32	2	5
Fountain	Iris	038	1	2	61	2	5
Freed	Nancy	039	1	2	36	3	6
Freeman	Vic	040	1	1	45	4	6
French	Charles	041	2	2	30	4	6
Fried	Harvey	042	2	2	58	5	8
Garrett	Helen	043	1	2	32	3	6
Gebhardt	Virginia	044	1	2	57	6	9
Gerken	Denise	045	1	1	24	1	6
Gillespie	Robbert	046	2	2	42	7	6
Golden	Jeff	047	2	2	35	2	5
Goode	Brad	048	2	2	36	2	5
Green	Paula	049	1	2	45	5	7
Gregory	Debbie	050	1	1	23	5	10
Haley	George	051	2	2	47	1	5
Hanson	Greg	052	2	1	50	3	7
Harding	Teresa	053	1	2	50	3	7
Henderson	Beverly	054	1	1	36	2	5
Hicks	Catharine	055	1	1	36	2	6
Horn	Ernest	056	2	2	57	7	8
Horner	Wilbur	057	2	2	39	7	6
Howard	Brian	058	2	2	55	6	7
Hubbard	Cheryl	059	1	2	42	7	5
Ivie	Marsha	060	1	1	39	5	7
Jackson	Charlie	061	2	2	27	5	8
Johnson	Herb	062	2	2	30	1	5
Johnston	Edwin	063	2	2	60	2	4
Jones	Nancy	064	1	1	33	2	7

Jordan	Clifton	065	2	1	21	3	7
Kimeldorf	Emily	066	1	2	25	5	7
Leaf	Bernice	067	1	2	36	4	6
Lee	Liz	068	1	2	39	5	7
Leiter	Ricky	069	2	2	23	5	7
Leonard	Cheryl	070	1	2	42	7	6
Lewin	Ronnie	071	2	2	31	1	5
Little	Annie	072	1	1	26	6	4
Lockley	Pam	073	1	1	45	6	7
Long	Peggy	074	1	2	57	7	6
Lyle	Sunny	075	2	2	50	7	5
Malone	Barbara	076	1	2	55	7	5
Marshall	Frank	077	2	2	19	1	4
Matthews	Bob	078	2	1	44	2	7
McCormick	Barbara	079	1	2	57	3	5
McDonald	Vera	080	1	2	52	4	4
Miller	Diane	081	1	2	31	5	8
Miller	Sam	082	2	2	48	5	10
Milligan	Guy	083	2	1	47	5	7
Mitchell	Donna	084	1	1	62	6	7
Moore	Michele	085	1	2	48	7	4
Morton	Jack	086	2	2	54	1	5
Nelson	Cynthia	087	1	2	60	2	7
Neugent	Will	088	2	2	20	3	6
Nielsen	Dudley	089	2	1	38	4	6
Nunn	Phil	090	2	1	35	5	7
Oliver	Dick	091	2	2	28	6	5
Owen	Monica	092	1	2	44	1	4
Page	Dorothy	093	1	2	50	1	5
Pearson	Calvin	094	2	2	40	2	7
Perry	Claude	095	2	2	45	3	7
Pettit	Janice	096	1	2	26	2	5
Phillips	Frank	097	2	2	38	4	5
Powell	Angie	098	1	1	27	5	8

Powers	Jerri	099	1	2	47	1	5
Rahn	Dean	100	2	2	59	2	4
Reeves	Tom	101	2	2	36	5	9
Renner	Martha	102	1	2	58	2	4
Roberts	Margie	103	1	2	56	2	4
Robertson	Helen	104	1	2	40	3	6
Robinson	Harvey	105	2	2	31	4	9
Rodman	Wes	106	2	2	50	6	6
Rogers	Kent	107	1	2	38	1	5
Rose	Debbie	108	1	2	46	5	9
Ross	Fran	109	1	2	20	1	4
Sanders	Mike	110	2	2	32	5	9
Saunders	Edith	111	1	2	46	1	5
Schmidt	Carrie	112	1	1	24	3	9
Schuster	Jean	113	1	1	52	5	7
Scott	Jay	114	2	2	56	3	7
Seagraves	Abraham	115	2	2	47	3	7
Sharpe	Alice	116	2	2	23	3	8
Shein	Ralph	117	2	2	33	6	7
Sherman	Myra	118	1	2	40	3	5
Simmons	Alex	119	2	2	28	3	8
Sims	Denise	120	1	2	53	2	5
Smith	Margie	121	1	2	40	4	5
Stillman	Billie	122	2	2	28	1	4
Stowe	Paula	123	1	2	52	1	6
Stuart	Jean	124	1	2	54	7	6
Sullivan	Joan	125	1	2	32	3	7
Summers	Linda	126	1	2	26	4	5
Taylor	Carol	127	1	2	28	2	6
Thomas	Jeff	128	2	2	45	3	5
Thompson	Lori	129	1	1	51	3	8
Tinsley	Brian	130	2	1	37	1	4
Tobias	Ron	131	2	2	41	5	8
Townsend	Anne	132	1	2	52	6	6

Tucker	Kay	133	1	2	45	4	9
Tupper	Jean	134	1	1	34	4	8
Van Cleve	Edith	135	1	2	31	4	7
Van Zandt	Howard	136	2	2	49	1	6
Vandell	Debbie	137	1	2	45	3	8
Wadley	Carla	138	1	2	22	3	8
Walker	Earl	139	2	2	59	4	6
Ward	Ron	140	2	1	55	5	9
Waters	Alan	141	2	1	24	1	4
Watson	Karen	142	1	2	43	6	8
Webster	Sam	143	2	2	21	1	5
Welch	Jeffrey	144	2	2	36	3	8
White	Suzanne	145	1	2	38	3	7
Whitt	Nancy	146	1	2	29	6	6
Wiggins	Harvey	147	2	2	59	2	6
Williams	Claudia	148	1	2	24	2	8
Wilson	Kathy	149	1	2	58	6	4
Wilson	Lee	150	2	2	20	7	4
Wolf	Jess	151	2	2	42	6	4
Wong	Sue	152	1	2	34	6	7
Wright	Beth	153	1	2	38	1	6
Yates	Alice	154	1	2	38	6	5
Zuccaro	Donald	155	2	1	42	1	3

Case Questions: Glenco Manufacturing

Name _____

1. Make your list of employees that you would recommend for the $500 bonus. Your list should contain approximately 20% of the employees.

1. _____	18. _____
2. _____	19. _____
3. _____	20. _____
4. _____	21. _____
5. _____	22. _____
6. _____	23. _____
7. _____	24. _____
8. _____	25. _____
9. _____	26. _____
10. _____	27. _____
11. _____	28. _____
12. _____	29. _____
13. _____	30. _____
14. _____	31. _____
15. _____	32. _____
16. _____	33. _____
17. _____	34. _____

2. Describe the statistical procedures you used and the results you obtained for developing your list of bonus recipients. Attach any relevant supporting output.

3. Explain why your procedures will result in the fair treatment of all employees at Glenco (*i.e.*, defend your reasoning for making those choices at the EBC meeting).

Baldwin Computer Sales

Baldwin Computer Sales is a small company located in Oldenburg, Washington. The founder of the company, Jonathan Baldwin, began the business by selling computer systems through mail-order at discount prices. Baldwin was one of the first computer mail-order companies to offer a toll-free phone number to their customers for support and trouble-shooting. While the company has grown over time, many new competitors have entered the computer mail-order marketplace so that Baldwin's share of this market has actually declined.

Five years ago, Bob Gravenstein, a marketing consultant, was contracted by Baldwin to develop long-term marketing plans and strategies for the company. After careful study, he recommended that Baldwin branch out to reach a new and growing segment of the computer sales market: college students. At that time, most universities were providing micro-computer labs and facilities for their students. However, many students were purchasing their own computers and printers so that they could have access to a computer at any time in their apartments or dorms. After graduation, students take the computers, with which they are already familiar, to their new jobs or use them at home after work hours. The percentage of college students owning a computer was increasing rapidly and Bob Gravenstein recommended that Baldwin Computer Sales take advantage of this marketing opportunity.

The marketing plan developed by Bob Gravenstein worked as follows: Five universities were initially selected for the program with expansion to other universities planned over time. Any student in at least his or her sophomore year at one of these universities was eligible to purchase a discounted JCN-2001 microcomputer system with printer from Baldwin Computer Sales under the program. The JCN-2001 is a private label, fully compatible system with all of the features of brand name models. The student makes a small payment each semester at the same time regular tuition payments were due. When the student graduates and finds a job, the payments are increased so that the computer will be paid for within two years after graduation. If the student fails to make payments at any time, Baldwin could repossess the computer system.

The prospect of future sales of computer equipment to these students was also part of the marketing strategy. The JCN-2001 is an entry-level computer system that suffices for most academic and professional uses. Eventually, however, many students who purchased this system would outgrow it and require an upgrade to a more powerful machine with more features. Bob Gravenstein argued that after their good experience with the JCN-2001, these customers would make their future purchases from Baldwin Computer Company.

Today, five years later, Baldwin Computer Sales is still operating the student purchase program and has expanded it to several more universities. There is currently enough data available from the early days of the program for Baldwin to determine whether or not the program has been successful and if it should be continued. To discuss the future of the student purchase program, Jonathan Baldwin has called a meeting with Ben Davis, who has been in charge of the program since it began, and Teresa Grimes, the new vice-president of marketing.

Baldwin: "I called you both in here today to discuss the student purchase program. As you know, the program has been in place for approximately five years and we need to make decisions about where to go from here. Ben, weren't you telling me last week that we now have enough data to evaluate the program?"

Davis: "Yes, sir. Any student who began the program as a sophomore five years ago should be out of school and employed for at least two years."

Baldwin: "Well, based on your information, would you say the program has been a success or a failure?"

Davis: "That's a tough call, sir. While most of the participants in the program eventually pay their account in full, we have had a high rate of defaults, some while the students were still in school, but mostly after they graduated."

Baldwin: "How much are we losing on those who default?"

Davis: "Each case is different. As I said, some default early and others after they have graduated. There are also the costs of repossession and repair to bring the product back up to resale quality. In many instances we were not able to retrieve the computer systems. Our data suggest that our average loss on each student-customer who defaults is about \$1,200. On the other hand, our average profit from participants who pay their accounts in full is approximately \$750. Overall, we are close to just breaking even."

Grimes: "Ben, have you considered 'qualifying' students for the program, much like a loan officer would qualify someone for a loan?"

Davis: "We had initially thought about doing that, but we didn't believe that there was much information, if any, in the way of a credit history on most college students. Applicants are still requested to provide as much information as possible on their application, including their class, grade point average, work experience, scholarships, and how much of their college expenses were earned through work. However, we weren't sure that this information was particularly useful for screening applicants."

Grimes: "Knowing that we were going to have this discussion today, I had one of my assistants who is well-versed in statistics look over some of those data last week. She has come up with a 'screening test' based only on the information you have been collecting from student applicants. By being more selective about whom we allow to participate in the student purchase program, it may be possible to increase our profit from the program."

Davis: "It would be easy enough to check out her screening test by trying it out on our early data from the program. In those cases, we know whether or not the student actually defaulted."

Baldwin: "Why don't the two of you spend some time on this idea and get back to me next week? At that time I want a recommendation to either discontinue the program, continue it as is, or continue it using this 'screening test' idea. Make sure you have the evidence to back up your recommendation."

Assignment

Ben Davis and Teresa Grimes must analyze the data from the student purchase program and make a recommendation to Mr. Baldwin about the future of the program. The necessary data are contained in the file BALDWIN.DAT on the Data Disk. The Data Description section contains a description of this data file.

Using this data set and other information given in the case, help Ben Davis and Teresa Grimes evaluate the student purchase program and recommend any necessary changes in the program. In particular, you need to evaluate the profitability of the program as it is currently administered and to evaluate the usefulness of the screening test developed by the assistant to Teresa Grimes. The Case Questions will assist you in your analysis of the data. Use important details from your analysis to support your recommendation.

Data Description

The data for the Baldwin Computer Sales case is contained in the file BALDWIN.DAT on the Data Disk. The file contains data on all participants in the student purchase program who by now should have either paid in full or defaulted (*i.e.*, those participants who should have graduated and held a job for at least two years). A partial listing of the data is shown below.

Student	School	Default	When	Score
6547	1	1	1	64
4503	2	0	0	58
1219	2	0	0	52
9843	4	1	0	56
6807	1	0	0	47
6386	4	0	0	58
⋮	⋮	⋮	⋮	⋮

These data are coded as follows:

Student: Student transaction number for identification purposes.

School: University where the student was enrolled.

Default: 1, in the event of default,
0, if account was paid in full on time.

When: 1, if default occurred (or paid in full) before graduation,
0, if default occurred (or paid in full) after graduation.

Score: Score on screening test based on student applicant information such as his or her class, grade point average, work experience, scholarships, and how much of their college expenses were earned through work.

Case Questions: Baldwin Computer Sales

Name _____

1. Estimate the probability that a customer participating in the student purchase program will default. Compute the expected profit from selling the JCN-2001 system to a university student under the existing program. Has the student purchase program been profitable? Explain and attach supporting output.

2. Based on the data, is defaulting on the computer payments independent of the university attended by the student? Show your work. (Hint: Realize that this is only a <u>sample</u> of data.) If there were dependence, what might be possible causes for this dependence?

3. Assume that 70 is a passing score on the screening test. Estimate the probability that a student who passes the screening test will eventually default. Compute the expected profit from selling the JCN-2001 system to a university student who passes the screening test. Is the screening test used in this fashion significantly better than not using the test at all? Explain your answer and attach any supporting output.

4. Can you find a better way of using the screening test that results in higher expected profits for Baldwin Computer Sales? Explain your solution and attach any relevant supporting output.

5. Make your final recommendation for the student purchase program to Jonathan Baldwin. Include any modifications that you would make to the program and discuss the potential changes caused by these modifications. Also discuss any other issues that should be considered.

Kilgore Manufacturing, Inc.

Kilgore Manufacturing, Inc. (KMI) is a small manufacturing company in the St. Louis area that produces components used in the aerospace industry. James Kilgore, the president and owner of KMI, started the company five years ago. Kilgore graduated with an electrical engineering degree from Georgia Tech and then went to work for Mitsuyo Electronics, another company with ties to the aerospace industry. In less than three years, he and another engineer at Mitsuyo left to start their own company which eventually became Kilgore Manufacturing. Although business has been reasonably steady for the last two years, KMI has yet to establish any long-term relationships with major aerospace contractors. This is important, because small companies like KMI only get business as subcontractors to the large aerospace manufacturing companies that win major contracts, many of which are with the federal government.

In the aerospace business, after the federal government approves a new defense project, a request for bids is sent to the major aerospace contractors, such as General Dynamics, McDonnell-Douglas, and Lockheed. Typically, many man-hours are devoted to the development of these bids. Submitted bids are evaluated and the contract is awarded to the company with the best proposal. This company, in turn, sends out a request for subcontractor bids to smaller companies like KMI for specific work related to the project. Often, the subcontract goes to the company with the lowest bid for the required work.

Cost overruns in federal government contracts are commonplace, but are becoming increasingly less accepted. The news media often report on projects in which the federal government, and therefore taxpayers, are severely overcharged. (In one widely publicized case, the government was charged $500 each for hammers!) In their desire to win subcontracts from the major aerospace companies, some subcontractors submit unreasonably low bids to perform the work on specific aspects of a major project. With hundreds of subcontractors ultimately winning a "piece of the pie" in the bidding process, the total dollar amount of underbidding on a major contract can be enormous. Of course, eventually all parties involved, including the taxpayers, find out about the cost overruns. Recently, the federal government has been cracking down severely on the major contractors, who in turn have demanded more accountability from their subcontractors. More and more contracts between the major contractor and its subcontractors are including harsher penalties for low production levels, late deliveries, cost overruns, and other failures by the subcontractors to meet the promises of their original bids.

Jim Kilgore has just learned that a new defense contract related to the Strategic Defense Initiative (SDI) has been awarded to one of the major aerospace contractors. A certain system in the project requires one of the components produced by KMI, a relay switch manufactured by only three other companies in the U.S. After finding out about the new contract, Kilgore held a strategy meeting with Tim Reynolds, vice-president of manufacturing, and Bill Shelton, plant manager.

Jim: "I don't know if you have heard yet, but a new SDI contract has been awarded to Avionics, Inc. The good news for us is that our R-7 relay switch plays a big role in the project. I think this is the opportunity we've been waiting for."

Tim: "How many units will Avionics need?"

Jim: "One of my contacts in Washington has given me enough information to estimate that the project will require at least 600 R-7 relay switches per day. But, my guess is that the subcontract will be awarded to the company that can provide the largest number of relay switches per day at the lowest cost to the government. Fortunately, our current contracts for the R-7 are about to run out so that we could devote that entire line of production to this new subcontract with Avionics. What do you think of this possibility, Bill?"

Bill: "We can easily meet the 600-per-day quota. Our production data over the past two years show an average daily production run of around 635 relay switches per day when we're running at full capacity."

Jim: "That's well and good, Bill, but we also need to know something about the amount of variability in daily production levels. In this new subcontract, we have to specify a guaranteed minimum level of daily production in addition to an average or typical daily production level. The government is really serious about contractors and subcontractors meeting their obligations. On those days we fall short of the guaranteed minimum, a $5,000 penalty is assessed!"

Tim: "$5,000! Ouch! Isn't that a little severe?"

Jim: "Unfortunately, we don't make the rules. However, we do want to play the game. Now, look, I want this contract; it's the break we've been looking for to get in solid with one of the key aerospace manufacturers. We can't afford, however, to lose money on this contract."

Bill: "Well, let's see what we know. Over the past two years, our lowest daily production run was 494 units and the highest was 768 units. In fact, if I remember right, the actual distribution of daily production levels is described fairly well by a normal distribution with a mean of about 635 units and a standard deviation of about 40 units."

Tim: "So there are definitely days when we are unable to make 600 units. If we were to bid 600 units, we would be hit with the $5,000 penalty from time to time. What sort of profit margin can we expect from Avionics, Jim?"

Jim: "I don't think that's going to be a problem. As best we can tell, our competitors are pretty close to us in terms of their production capabilities and production costs. As a result, I think we can maintain our usual profit margin of $3.80 per relay switch. It really boils down to who can produce the most relay switches daily. But we have to be very careful with our bid. Bid too low on the guaranteed minimum daily number of units and we lose the contract to one of our competitors; bid too high and we get the contract, but we lose our shirts in penalties."

Tim: "Let me make sure I understand the situation. Suppose, for example, that we were to guarantee a minimum daily production level of 600 units, but we fell short, say 5% of the time. Then, by my calculations, we would net an average daily profit of $2,163."

Jim: "Whoa! Slow down! How did you come up with that figure?"

Tim: "Well, each day's production level will be different and there is no way we can predict when we will fall short of the guaranteed bid level, but we can still talk in terms of averages. Going back to my example, suppose we fall short 5% of the time. We would incur the $5,000 penalty about once in every 20 days which averages out to $250 per day. If we actually average 635 relay switches per day, then over a typical 20-day period we would produce about 12,700 relay switches. At a $3.80 profit margin, the average profit for a 20-day period would be $48,260, which comes to $2,413 per day. After subtracting the $5,000 penalty for one day out of the twenty, our average net daily profit over the 20 days drops to $2,163."

Bill: "Where did the 5% figure come from?"

Tim: "I just made it up for the example. It should be pretty close to correct, but I'm not sure."

Jim: "Good job! That's a great example of how to think through this problem. Of course, everything depends on how often we fall short and that is determined by our guaranteed bid level."

Tim: "You know, one way we could cut out some of the penalty costs would be to stockpile relay switches on those days that we produce more than the guaranteed bid level."

Jim: "Nice idea, Tim. I had already thought of that but then found out from Avionics that we have to turn over our entire production to them each day. Besides, we don't have the space for inventory."

Bill: "And we can't use any overtime to meet the minimum when we are just short because we will be operating 24 hours a day with our three shifts. If we borrow a little from the next day's production to meet the minimum, we stand a higher chance of not meeting the minimum the next day."

Jim: "That's right. So in our calculations to come up with a guaranteed minimum daily level of production, we need to assume that we sell everything we produce each day, that we cannot stockpile or create a stand-by inventory, and that we can't use any overtime or borrow from later production to avoid a penalty."

Bill: "When do we have to submit the bid?"

Jim: "That's the good news. The deadline for submitting a bid is approximately three months away."

Bill: "Great! Here's why I ask. A new worker in the plant suggested some changes to our R-7 production process during one of our quality circle meetings last week. I think the idea's a winner. These changes would result in a more complicated production process with a steep learning curve for the workers, but it could eventually lead to higher production levels. Here's the best part. We can do it with only minor modifications to our current equipment and it will cost practically nothing to make the changes! We could implement the new procedure in less than a week's time."

Jim: "This could be what we need to pull off this deal. Bill, start making the necessary changes. We'll monitor production levels for the next 60 production days. If the new process works as you suggest, we should see higher production in the second 30-day cycle. If so, we'll make our bid based on the new process; otherwise, we'll switch back to the old procedure and base our bid on the data from the past two years."

Tim: "Getting back to profits again, how much profit do we really need to make in order to pursue this contract?"

Jim: "I can't overemphasize the importance of this contract to us. If we are awarded the contract and do a good job, it could lead to a long-term relationship with Avionics and would certainly enhance our reputation with other major aerospace companies. We can't afford to lose money on this contract. I'd be willing to break even just to get these nonmonetary benefits, but we can't. I'll tell you what, if we could just make $1,000 per day on this job, the accountants and I would be happy. Bill, report back in 60 days to let us know how the new production plan is working. The three of us will assess the situation at that time and develop the bid proposal."

Assignment

During the next 60 days of production, Bill Shelton keeps track of daily production levels of the R-7 relay switch after making the changes to the manufacturing process suggested by one of the workers. The data are contained in the file KILGORE.DAT on the Data Disk. Appendix A contains a description of this data file.

Using this data set and other information given in the case, help Jim Kilgore determine how to bid for the R-7 relay switch contract with Avionics. In particular, you need to decide whether to go with the old or the new R-7 production process and then determine what the guaranteed minimum daily production level should be. The Case Questions will assist you in your analysis of the data. Use important details from your analysis to support your recommendation.

Data Description

The data for the Kilgore Manufacturing case is contained in the file KILGORE.DAT on the data disk. The file contains data for the first 60 days of production under the new manufacturing process implemented at KMI for producing the R-7 relay switch. A partial listing of the data is shown below.

Month	Date	Units Produced
6	3	524
6	4	559
6	5	557
6	6	549
6	7	598
6	10	572
⋮	⋮	⋮

These data are coded as follows:

Month: Month of production for that production day (6 = June, 7 = July, and 8 = August).

Date: Date of the month for that production day.

Units Produced: Number of units produced on that day.

Case Questions: Kilgore Manufacturing, Inc.

Name _____

1. Calculate the guaranteed minimum daily production level under the <u>existing</u> production process that will result in an average net daily profit of $1,000, the amount needed by KMI. Show all work.

2. On what percentage of production days will KMI incur a penalty if they bid this number of units? Show all work.

3. Analyze the distribution of daily production levels under the <u>new</u> production process suggested by one of the workers.

    a. What are the mean and standard deviation? How do these values compare to the mean and standard deviation of daily production under the existing method?

    b. Does a normal distribution seem appropriate for the daily production levels under the new method? If not, how would you describe the shape of this data distribution?

4. Bill Shelton said that the workers would most likely have a steep learning curve with the <u>new</u> production process.

   a. Do the data support his claim? What numerical and/or graphical summaries of the data are useful in checking out this claim of a learning effect? Attach any relevant supporting output.

   b. Based on your findings, what would you suggest as the next step in the analysis of these data?

5. Under the <u>new</u> production process, what guaranteed minimum daily production level would you recommend that KMI propose in their bid? Explain your answer and show your work. Support any assumptions with evidence from the data analysis where possible.

6. Make your final recommendation to KMI. What should they bid to get the contract with Avionics?

Pronto Pizza

Pronto Pizza is a family-owned pizza restaurant in Vinemont, a small town of 20,000 people in upstate New York. Antonio Scapelli started the business 30 years ago as Antonio's Restaurant with just a few thousand dollars. Antonio, his wife, and their children, most of whom are now grown, operate the business. Several years ago, one of Antonio's sons, Tony, Jr., graduated from NYU with an undergraduate degree in business administration. After graduation, he came back to manage the family business. Pronto Pizza was one of the earliest pizza restaurants to offer pizza delivery to homes. Fortunately, Tony had the foresight to make this business decision a few years ago. At the same time, he changed the restaurant's name from Antonio's to Pronto Pizza to emphasize the pizza delivery service. The restaurant has thrived since then, and has become one of the leading businesses in the area. While many of their customers still "dine-in" at the restaurant, nearly 90% of Pronto's current business is derived from the pizza delivery service.

Recently, one of the national-chain fast food pizza delivery services found its way to Vinemont, New York. In order to attract business, this new competitor has guaranteed delivery of its pizzas within 30 minutes after the order is placed. If the delivery is not made within 30 minutes, the customer receives the order without charge. Before long, there were signs that this new pizza restaurant was taking business away from Pronto Pizza. Tony realized that Pronto Pizza would have to offer a similar guarantee in order to remain competitive.

After a careful cost analysis, Tony determined that to offer a guarantee of 29 minutes or less, Pronto's average delivery time would have to be 25 minutes or less. Tony thought that this would limit the percentage of "free pizzas" under the guarantee to about 5% of all deliveries, which he had figured to be the break-even point for such a promotion. To be sure of Pronto's ability to deliver on a promise of 29 minutes or less, Tony knew that he needed to collect data on Pronto's pizza deliveries.

Pronto Pizza's delivery service operates from 4:00 p.m. to midnight every day of the week. After an order for a pizza is phoned in, one of the two cooks is given the order for preparation. When the crust is prepared and the ingredients have been added, the pizza is placed on the belt of the conveyor oven. The speed of the conveyor is set so that pizzas come out perfectly, time after time. Once the pizza is ready and one of Pronto's drivers is available to make the delivery, the pizza is taken in a heat-insulated bag to the customer. Pronto uses approximately five to six drivers each night for deliveries. Most of the drivers hired by Pronto Pizza are juniors and seniors at the local high school.

Given the large number of deliveries made each evening, Tony knew that he could not possibly monitor every single delivery. He had thought of the possibility of having someone else collect the data, but given the importance of accurate data, he decided to make all of the measurements himself. This, of course, meant taking a random sample of, rather than all, deliveries over some time period. Tony decided to monitor deliveries over the course of a full month. During each hour of delivery service operation, he randomly selected a phoned-in order. He then carefully measured the time required to prepare the order and the amount of time that the order had to wait for a delivery person to become available. Tony would then go with the delivery person to accurately measure the delivery time. After returning, Tony randomly selected an order placed during the next hour and repeated the process. At the end of the month, Tony had collected data on 240 deliveries.

Once the data were available, Tony knew there were several issues that should be addressed. He was committed to going with the 29-minute delivery guarantee unless the data strongly indicated that the true average delivery time was greater than 25 minutes. How would he make this decision? Tony also realized that there were three components that could affect pizza delivery times: the preparation time, the waiting time for an available driver, and the travel time to deliver the pizza to the customer. Tony hoped that he had collected sufficient data to allow him to determine how he might improve the delivery operation by reducing the overall delivery time.

Assignment

Tony has asked you for some assistance in interpreting the data that he has collected. In particular, he needs to know if the true average delivery time for Pronto Pizza is greater than 25 minutes. Use the data in the file PRONTO.DAT on the Data Disk to answer his question. A description of this data set is given in the Data Description section. Also, examine the data for further information that might help Tony in making his decision about the 29-minute delivery guarantee and in improving his pizza delivery service. The Case Questions will assist you in your analysis of the data. Use important details from your analysis to support your recommendations.

Data Description

The PRONTO.DAT file on the Data Disk contains the data collected by Tony Scapelli over the past month on pizza deliveries. Data are recorded for each delivery order placed in the manner depicted below.

DAY	HOUR	PREP TIME	WAIT TIME	TRAVEL TIME	DISTANCE
5	4	14.86	3.08	6.02	2.5
5	5	14.84	13.81	5.47	3.3
5	6	15.41	9.91	8.99	4.9
5	7	16.34	2.08	7.98	3.8
5	8	15.19	2.69	9.01	4.9
⋮	⋮	⋮	⋮	⋮	⋮

The variables are defined as follows:

DAY: Day of the week (1=Monday, 7=Sunday).

HOUR: Hour of the day (4-11 p.m.).

PREP TIME: Time required (in minutes) to prepare the order.

WAIT TIME: Time (in minutes) from completing preparation of the order until a delivery person was available to deliver the order.

TRAVEL TIME: Time (in minutes) it took the car to reach the delivery location.

DISTANCE: Distance (in miles) from Pronto Pizza to the delivery location.

Case Questions: Pronto Pizza

Name _____

1. Is there sufficient evidence in the data to conclude that the average time to deliver a pizza, once the order is placed, is greater than 25 minutes? Perform an appropriate statistical analysis and attach any supporting output.

2. What percentage of the time will Pronto fail to meets its guaranteed time of 29 minutes or less? Explain how you arrived at your answer and discuss any assumptions that you are making. Will they meet their requirement of failing to meet the guarantee 5% of the time or less?

3. Does the day of the week have an effect on delivery time? Attach any supporting output for your answer.

4. Does the time of day have an effect on delivery time? Attach any supporting output for your answer.

5. Discuss Tony Scapelli's data design and collection. Comment on any potential problems resulting from the way in which the data were collected. Would you recommend that he collect additional data in order to better evaluate the pizza delivery service? Explain.

6. Based on your analysis of the data, what action (or actions) would you recommend to the owners of Pronto Pizza to improve their operation? Attach any supporting output that led to your conclusion.

DataStor Company

"Another rejected shipment!" exclaimed Bill Roberts. "That makes four in the past twenty days!" Tony Escalera knew that Roberts would not take the news well. Something was wrong, and things were going to be uncomfortable for everybody at DataStor until the problem was resolved.

DataStor produces magnetic data storage devices and media for the computer industry. A few years ago, they began producing the DataStor DS1000, a compact hard drive with the capability of storing 1 gigabyte (1,000 megabytes) of information. Most of the drives they produce are sold to companies that resell the drives under their own product label to consumers and commercial businesses. DataStor's main buyer is Four-D Office Products. Four-D is a national retailer that sells the drives under its own product label to final consumers and some computer companies. This arrangement with Four-D has been very profitable for DataStor.

Bill Roberts has been vice-president in charge of sales at DataStor for the past four years. His rapid rise up the company's management ladder was due in large part to his role in developing the partnership with Four-D Office Products. Four-D was impressed with Roberts and DataStor's commitment to quality.

In the DataStor DS1000 hard drive manufacturing process, each of the three 8-hour shifts produces approximately 120 drives per day. As part of the quality inspection process, one drive is sampled each hour and subjected to the PDQ (Performance and Drive Quality) test, originally developed by DataStor. The PDQ is a rigorous test of a hard drive that measures the performance of the drive in a variety of conditions, checks the accuracy and speed of the drive in storing and retrieving information, and tests for defects in the drive's mechanism and storage media. The PDQ is a relatively expensive test and takes up to twenty minutes to complete. At the conclusion of the test, an overall test score based on drive characteristics is computed. PDQ test scores for the hard drives produced at DataStor have historically followed a normal distribution with a mean value of 7.0 and a standard deviation of .30 when the process has been in control. Each hour, the new PDQ value is added to a control chart used in monitoring the process for early detection of drive quality problems. Signals from test scores below the lower control limit (LCL) may indicate a drop in quality, while signals from test scores above the upper control limit (UCL) may indicate a potential improvement in the process.

Shipments of DataStor DS1000 hard drives are made to Four-D once each day. Before Four-D accepts a shipment, they subject a random sample of 10 drives to the PDQ test as a final inspection. At Four-D, a drive is judged to be nonconforming if its performance test score falls below 6.2. If one or more drives in the sample of 10 are found to be nonconforming, the entire shipment is judged to be "unacceptable" and returned to DataStor. Under the arrangement with Four-D, DataStor is required to pay a penalty to Four-D and must replace the unacceptable shipment within 24 hours. Further penalties are assessed for each additional day that passes before the shipment is replaced.

The production engineers at DataStor have told Bill Roberts that "zero-defect" production is virtually impossible, but that the percentage of defects has been reduced to the point that only rarely will a shipment be judged unacceptable. In recent weeks, however, there has been a noticeable increase in the frequency of returned shipments from Four-D. Tony Escalera, the chief production engineer at DataStor, brought word of the latest returned shipment to Bill Roberts.

Roberts: "Another rejected shipment! That makes four in the past twenty days! What's going on, Tony?"

Escalera: "At this point, I don't know any more than you do, Mr. Roberts. To borrow some statistical terminology, it's possible that we're just experiencing a few 'false rejections.' After all, there is variability in any process. Even if the actual quality levels are on target, we expect a few inspections to indicate otherwise."

Roberts: "The number of rejections still seems to be much higher than we have experienced in the past. Do you think that Four-D has become more demanding in their acceptable level of quality?"

Escalera: "That's possible, but surely they would have let us know first. Maybe they are making mistakes when they conduct the PDQ tests or when they interpret the results."

Roberts: "Or maybe we're the ones making the mistakes. Do we have evidence of any quality problems here?"

Escalera: "As you know, we sample one drive each hour of each shift and run the PDQ test. In the past, we plotted the individual test scores on a control chart to monitor the process for early warning signals of problems. Recently, though, we began plotting the average of the eight PDQ test values collected over each shift on our charts instead of the individual values. Our new quality control person told us that this approach should result in a more sensitive warning system."

Roberts: "Have your control charts indicated any problems?"

Escalera: "No. As you can tell from this latest two-sigma control chart, there have not been any out of control signals in the past 150 shifts. That's actually a surprising performance record. We would normally expect about seven or eight values out of 150 to fall outside the two-sigma control limits. If anything, it looks like the variability in process quality is much lower than it has been in the past."

Control Chart for Shift Average PDQ Test Scores

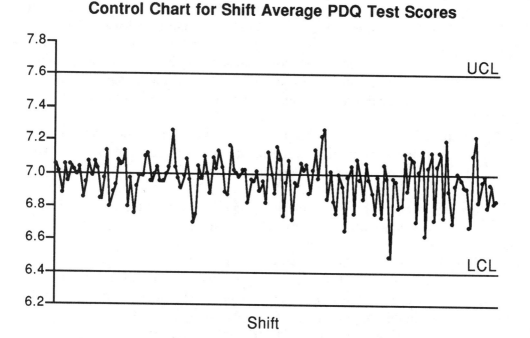

Shift

Roberts: "Yes, but if the variability has actually decreased, why haven't we seen <u>fewer</u> returned shipments? Are we plotting and interpreting these shift averages on the charts correctly?"

Escalera: "I think so. I'll go back and let the quality control person take a look at what we've been doing."

Roberts: "Maybe the problem really is at Four-D. Wait a minute! We're forgetting something. If everything looks good on our end, but Four-D is finding nonconformances in our shipments, could the problem be due to damage during shipment?"

Escalera: "Someone else suggested that possibility to me earlier. But it's pretty unlikely given the protective packaging we use."

Roberts: "Tony, we need to resolve this problem, if there is one, as quickly as possible. Check out our side first for the source of the problem. If you can't turn up anything here, make some inquiries with your contacts at Four-D."

Assignment

The data from the drive quality tests conducted at DataStor over the past 150 shifts are contained in the file DATASTOR.DAT on the Data Disk. The Data Description section contains a description of this data file.

Using this data set and other information given in the case, help Bill Roberts and Tony Escalera solve the quality problem they are experiencing at DataStor. In particular, speculate as to the source of the problem based on your analysis of the data. The Case Questions will assist you in your analysis of the data. Use important details from your analysis to support your recommendation.

Data Description

The data for the DataStor Company case is contained in the file DATASTOR.DAT on the Data Disk. The file contains performance testing data on the DataStor DS1000 hard drives produced over the past 150 shifts. A partial listing of the data is shown below.

Week	Day	Shift	Hours	Drives	Shift PDQ
1	1	1	91.75	111	7.052
1	1	2	91.25	115	7.010
1	1	3	103.75	128	6.884
1	2	1	96.75	123	7.051
1	2	2	103.25	128	6.952
1	2	3	91.50	115	7.049
⋮	⋮	⋮	⋮	⋮	⋮

These data are coded as follows:

Week: Week (1–10).

Day: 1 = Monday, 2 = Tuesday, 3 = Wednesday, 4 = Thursday, and 5 = Friday.

Shift: 1, if first shift,
2, if second shift,
3, if third shift.

Hours: Total number of hours worked by production employees during the shift.

Drives: Number of DataStor DS1000 hard drives produced during the shift.

Shift PDQ: The average PDQ test score recorded for the eight drives tested during the shift. One randomly selected drive is tested each hour of every shift.

Case Questions: DataStor Company

Name _____

1. If the DataStor DS1000 hard drive production process at DataStor Company is in control, what percentage of the drives produced would be considered in nonconformance by Four-D?

2. If the DataStor DS1000 hard drive production process at DataStor Company is in control, how often would shipments be found unacceptable by Four-D?

3. What is the probability of four rejected shipments in the past twenty days assuming that the process has been in control all this time?

4. Speculate as to the source of the problem at DataStor Company. Has the problem with unaccepted shipments been due to an increase in drive nonconformances at DataStor, to increased quality requirements by Four-D Office Products, to damage during shipment, or is it simply due to random variation? Be as specific as possible. What evidence leads you to your conclusion? Attach any supporting evidence from your data analysis.

Easton Realty Company

Sam Easton started out as a real estate agent in Atlanta ten years ago. After working two years for a national real estate firm, he transferred to Dallas, Texas and worked for another realty agency. His friends and relatives convinced him that with his experience and knowledge of the real estate business, he should open his own agency. He eventually acquired his broker's license and before long started his own company, Easton Realty, in Fort Worth. Two salespeople at the previous company agreed to follow him to the new company. Easton currently has eight real estate agents working for him. Before the real estate slump, the combined residential sales for Easton Realty amounted to approximately $15 million annually.

Recently, the Dallas-Fort Worth metroplex and the state of Texas have suffered economic problems from several sources. Much of the wealth in Texas was generated by the oil industry, but the oil industry has fallen on hard times in recent years. Many savings and loan (S&L) institutions loaned large amounts of money to the oil industry and to commercial and residential construction. As the oil industry fell off and the economy weakened, many S&L's found themselves in difficulty as a result of poor real estate investments and the soft real estate market that was getting worse with each passing month. With the lessening of the Cold War, less federal money was being spent on defense. The federal government closed several military bases across the country including two in the DFW area. Large government contractors, such as General Dynamics, had to trim down their operations and lay off many workers. This added more pressure to the real estate market by putting more houses on an already saturated market. Real estate agencies found it more difficult with each passing month to sell houses.

Two days ago, Sam Easton received a special delivery letter from the president of the local Board of Realtors. The Board had received complaints from two people who had listed and sold their homes through Easton Realty in the past month. The president of the Board of Realtors was informing Sam of these complaints and giving him the opportunity to respond. Both complaints were triggered by a recent article on home sales appearing in one of the local newspapers. The article contained the table shown below.

Typical Home Sale in the DFW Area

Average Sales Price	$ 104,250
Average Size	1860 sq. ft.

Note: Includes all homes sold in Dallas, Fort Worth, Arlington, and the MidCities over the past 12 months.

The two sellers charged that Easton Realty had underpriced their homes in order to accelerate the sales. The first house is located in Arlington, is four years old, has 2190 square feet, and sold for $88,500. The second house is located in Fort Worth, is nine years old, has 1848 square feet, and sold for $79,500. Both houses in question are three-bedroom houses. Both sellers believe that they would have received more money for their houses if Easton Realty had priced them at their true market value.

Sam knew from experience that people selling their homes invariably overestimate the value. Most sellers believe they could have gotten more money from the sale of their homes. But Sam also knew that his agents would not intentionally underprice houses. However, in these bad economic times, many real estate companies, including Easton Realty, had large inventories of houses for sale and needed to make sales. One quick way to unload these houses is to underprice them. On a residential sale, an agent working under a real estate broker typically makes about 3% of the sales price if he originally listed the property. Dropping the sales price of a $100,000 home down to $90,000 would speed up the sale and the agent's commission would only fall from $3,000 to $2,700. Some real estate agents might consider sacrificing $300 in order to get their commission sooner, but it is unethical because the agent is supposed to be representing the seller and acting in the seller's best interests. Sam had to convince the two sellers and the Board of Realtors that there was no substance to the complaints. The question was how was he going to do it?

First, he needed to obtain recent residential sales data. Unfortunately, the local MLS (multiple listing service) did not contain actual sales prices of homes. However, Pat McCloskey, a local real estate appraiser, did maintain a data base that had the sales information Sam needed. Phoning Pat, Sam found that she indeed had the data he required, but she would have to merge her personal database with data downloaded from the MLS in order to give Sam the necessary information. Fortunately, this was a relatively simple task and Pat could get the data on a disk to Sam the next day.

Sam asked Pat to give him all the data she had on home sales that had taken place in the DFW area over the previous four months. While Pat's database did not contain all home sales in the DFW metroplex over that period of time, the data she had were representative of the entire population. The data for each home sold included the sale month, the sale price, the size of the home (in square feet of heated floor space), the number of bedrooms, the age of the house, the area within the DFW metroplex where the house is located, and the real estate company that sold the home.

Assignment

The real estate data compiled by Pat McCloskey for Sam Easton are contained in the file EASTON.DAT on the Data Disk. The Data Description section provides a partial listing of this data file along with definitions of the variables. Using this data set and other information given in the case, help Sam Easton show that the underpricing claims of his former clients are not true. First, you should determine whether or not the two houses in question were underpriced relative to the market, *i.e.*, relative to comparable houses sold by other realtors. Secondly, you need to determine whether or not Easton has been underpricing houses relative to its competitors. The Case Questions will assist you in your analysis of the data. Use important details from your analysis of the data to support your recommendation.

Data Description

The data for the Easton Realty case is contained in the file EASTON.DAT on the Data Disk. The file contains data on home sales over the past four months in the DFW area. A partial listing of the data is shown below. (See the Important Note below.)

Month	Price	Size	Bedrooms	Age	Area	Agency
3	82400	1800	3	3	2	0
3	72800	1362	2	7	2	0
3	90000	1819	3	6	2	1
3	67600	1594	3	7	3	0
⋮	⋮	⋮	⋮	⋮	⋮	⋮

The variables are defined as follows:

Month: Month in which the sale took place:
3, if March,
4, if April,
5, if May,
6, if June.

Price: Sale price of the house in dollars.

Size: Square feet of heated floor space.

Bedrooms: Number of bedrooms in the house.

Age: Age of the house in years.

Area: Area in the DFW metroplex where the house is located:
1, if Dallas,
2, if Fort Worth,
3, if elsewhere in the metroplex.

Agency: 1, if Easton Realty Company sold the house,
0, otherwise.

IMPORTANT NOTE: Due to the size of the data file EASTON.DAT, some student versions of statistical software packages may not be capable of analyzing this data set. Consult your instructor if you have any problems.

Case Questions: Easton Realty Company

Name _____

1. First consider the claim that the two houses in question did not sell for
   their fair market value.

   a. Compare the selling prices of the two houses to the average selling
      price of all houses sold in the four-month period. Does the
      difference appear to be substantial? Explain using the data and
      summary statistics to support your statements. Attach any relevant
      supporting output.

   b. Provide at least three reasons why the comparison in part (a) is not
      fair, *i.e.*, describe factors impacting on sales prices that are not taken
      into account in drawing the comparison in part (a).

c. Use the data to present an accurate and fair comparison of the selling prices of two houses to other home sales. Were the two houses underpriced? Explain. Attach any relevant supporting output.

2. Now consider the claim that Easton Realty Company has been under-pricing its residential properties relative to other real estate companies.

   a. Use numerical and graphical summaries to compare the pricing by Easton and other realtors. Attach computer output to this page and briefly describe your findings below.

b. Conduct a fair and accurate statistical analysis of the difference between pricing by Easton and other realtors. Attach any relevant supporting output to this page and summarize the results below. Is Easton underpricing relative to the other realtors?

c. Prepare a brief, convincing response to the claims of underpricing.

Circuit Systems, Inc.

Circuit Systems, Incorporated is a company located in Northern California that produces integrated circuit boards for the microcomputer industry. In addition to salaried management and office staff personnel, Circuit Systems currently employs approximately 250 hourly production workers involved in the actual assembly of the circuit boards. These hourly employees earn an average of $11.00 per hour.

Thomas Nelson, the Director of Human Resources at Circuit Systems, has been concerned with hourly employee absenteeism within the company. Presently, each hourly employee earns eighteen days of paid sick leave per year. Thomas has found that many of these employees use most or all of their sick leave well before the year is over. After an informal survey of employee records, Thomas is convinced that while most hourly employees make legitimate use of their sick leave, there are many who view paid sick leave as "extra" vacation time and "call in sick" when they want to take off from work. This has been a source of conflict between the hourly production workers and management. The problem is due in part to a restrictive vacation policy at Circuit Systems in which hourly employees receive only one week of paid vacation per year in addition to a few paid holidays. With only one week of paid vacation and a few paid holidays, the hourly production employees work a 50-week year, not counting paid sick leave.

In an effort to save money and increase productivity, Thomas has developed a two-point plan that was recently approved by the president of Circuit Systems. To combat the abuse of paid sick leave, hourly workers will now be allowed to convert unused paid sick leave to cash on a "three-for-one" basis, *i.e.*, each unused day of sick leave can be converted into an additional one-third of a day's pay. An hourly employee could earn up to an additional six days of pay each year if he or she does not take any paid sick leave during the year. Even though a worker could gain more time off by dishonestly "phoning in sick," Thomas hopes that the majority of hourly employees will view this approved conversion of sick leave into extra pay as a more acceptable alternative. In the second part of his plan, Thomas is instituting a voluntary exercise program for hourly employees to improve their overall health. At an annual company expense of $200 for each hourly employee who participates, Circuit Systems will subsidize membership in a local health club. In return, the participating employee is required to exercise at least three times per week outside of regular working hours to maintain his or her free membership. At no cost to Circuit Systems, the company's health insurance carrier has also agreed to reduce the monthly premiums of those employees who participate in the exercise program and are non-smokers (or have quit smoking). In fact, in the long term, an investment in employees' physical well-being is expected to substantially reduce the company's contribution to health insurance premiums. In discussions with hourly employees, Thomas has found that many of them approve of the exercise program and are willing to participate.

Many of the supervisors that Thomas has spoken with believe that the paid sick leave conversion and the exercise program may help in curbing the absenteeism problem, but others did not give it much hope for succeeding and thought the cost would outweigh any benefits. The president of Circuit Systems agreed to give the proposal a one-year trial period. At the end of the trial period, Thomas must evaluate the new anti-absenteeism plan, present the results, and make a recommendation to either continue or discontinue the plan.

Assignment

Over the next year, during which time the sick leave conversion and exercise program are in place, Thomas Nelson maintains data on employee absences, use of the sick leave conversion privilege, participation in the exercise program, and other pertinent information. He has also gone back to collect data from the year prior to starting the new program in order to evaluate the new program. The data are in the file CIRCUIT.DAT on the Data Disk. The Data Description section contains a description of this data file.

Using this data set and other information given in the case, help Thomas Nelson evaluate the new program to determine if it is effective in reducing the average cost of absenteeism by hourly employees, thereby increasing worker productivity. In particular, you need to compare this year's data to last year's data to determine if there has been a reduction in the average cost of absenteeism per hourly production worker by going to the new program. The Case Questions will assist you in your analysis of the data. Use important details from your analysis to support your recommendation.

Data Description

The data for the Circuit Systems case is contained in the file CIRCUIT.DAT on the Data Disk. The file contains data for the past two years on hourly production employees in the company who were with the company for that entire period of time. A partial listing of the data is shown below.

Employee	Hourly Pay	Sick Leave Last Year	Sick Leave This Year	Exercise Program
6631	10.97	3.50	2.00	0
7179	11.35	24.00	12.50	0
2304	10.75	18.00	12.75	0
9819	10.96	21.25	14.00	0
4479	10.59	16.50	11.75	0
1484	11.41	16.50	9.75	1
⋮	⋮	⋮	⋮	⋮

These data are coded as follows:

Employee:	Employee ID number.
Hourly Pay:	Hourly pay of the employee in both years. Unfortunately, due to economic conditions, there were no pay raises last year.
Sick Leave Last Year:	Actual number of days of sick leave taken by the employee last year before the new program started.
Sick Leave This Year:	Actual number of days of sick leave taken by the employee this year under the new program.
Exercise Program:	1, if participating in the exercise program, 0, if not participating.

Case Questions: Circuit Systems, Inc.

Name _____

1. Keeping in mind that reducing the average cost of absenteeism by hourly workers is the goal, carefully define the variable(s) by which you will measure the effectiveness of the new anti-absenteeism program. Explain your choice.

2. Use appropriate statistical techniques to evaluate the effectiveness of the anti-absenteeism program. Discuss the statistical and the practical significance of the results. Attach all relevant output.

3. Is there any evidence that the exercise program has been effective in reducing paid sick leave taken by hourly production employees? Use appropriate statistical tools to support your conclusions. Discuss the results and attach any relevant supporting output.

4. How much did the anti-absenteeism program save or lose this year? Construct a table comparing this year's results under the new program to last year's results before the program was implemented. Give a breakdown that shows the costs of the unused sick leave conversion and the exercise program.

5. Make your final recommendations about the anti-absenteeism program. Include any modifications that you would make to the program and discuss the potential changes, if any, caused by these modifications.

Fastest Courier in the West

The law firm of Adams, Babcock, and Connors is located in the Dallas-Fort Worth metroplex. Randall Adams is the senior and founding partner in the firm. John Babcock has been a partner in the firm for the past eight years, and Blake Connors became a partner just last year. The firm employs two paralegal assistants and three secretaries. In addition, Bill Davis, the newly hired office manager, is in charge of day-to-day operations and manages the financial affairs of the law firm.

A major aspect of the law firm's business is the preparation of contracts and other legal documents for their clients. A courier service is employed by the firm to deliver legal documents to their many clients as they are scattered throughout the metroplex. The downtown centers of Dallas and Fort Worth are separated by a distance of approximately 30 miles. With the large sizes of these cities and their associated heavy traffic, a trip by car from the southwest side of Fort Worth to the northeast side of Dallas can easily take longer than an hour. Due to the importance of the legal documents involved, their timely delivery is a high priority item. At a recent partner's meeting, the topic of courier delivery came up.

Adams: "Recently, we have received a couple of complaints from some of our best clients about delayed contract deliveries. I spent the better part of an hour yesterday afternoon trying to calm down old man Dixon. He claims that if those contracts had arrived any later, his deal with the Taguchi Group would have fallen through."

Connors:	"Well, it wasn't our fault. Anne had the contracts all typed and proofread before nine in the morning."
Adams:	"No, no. Everything was handled fine on our end. The delay was the courier's fault. Something about a delay in the delivery..."
Babcock:	"Metro Delivery has always done a good job for us in the past. I am sure that these are just a few unusual incidents."
Connors:	"On the other hand, it could be an indication that their service is slipping."
Adams:	"In any event, we cannot afford to offend our clients. No one is perfect, but it only takes one or two bad incidents to lose important clients. At least two new courier services that have opened in the metroplex during the last two years. I hear good things about them from some of my friends. The question is: Should we keep using Metro or consider using one of these other services?"
Connors:	"How would you suggest that we make this decision?"
Babcock:	"Why not give each one a trial period and choose the best performer?"
Adams:	"Great idea! But how would you decide who's best?"
Babcock:	"Well, obviously the choice boils down to picking the fastest courier service. Given our recent problem, we also want to avoid the infrequent, but costly, delayed deliveries. Delivery cost is an important secondary criterion."
Connors:	"Why not let our new office manager run this little "contest" for a few weeks? Bill normally keeps fairly detailed information about contract deliveries anyway. As the need for deliveries arises, he can rotate through all three couriers."
Adams:	"Let's be sure not to let any of the couriers know about the contest; otherwise, we may not see their typical performance.

We'll take up this topic again after Bill has collected and analyzed some data and is ready to make a presentation."

During the past month, Bill Davis has kept detailed records of the deliveries made by each of three courier services: DFW Express, Carborne Carrier, and Metro Delivery (the courier presently used by the law firm). Due to the importance of the documents delivered, a courier is required to phone the law office as soon as a delivery has been made at its destination. For each delivery, Bill's data set contains: the courier used, the pickup time, the delivery time, the mileage of the delivery, and the cost of the delivery. Each of the courier services charges a flat fee plus a mileage charge for each delivery. These charges vary from courier to courier.

Assignment

As office manager, Bill Davis is responsible for making the decision as to which courier service will be given the exclusive contract. Using the data set stored in the file COURIER.DAT on your Data Disk, assist Bill in choosing among the three courier services and defending his choice to the partners of the firm by performing a statistical analysis of the data. Write a short report to the partners giving your final recommendation. The Case Questions will assist you in your analysis of the data. Use important details from your analysis of the data to support your recommendation.

Data Description

For each delivery, Bill Davis' data set contains the courier used, the pickup time, the delivery time, the mileage of the delivery, and the cost of the delivery. The first few entries in the database are shown below. The entire database is in the file COURIER.DAT on the Data Disk. It contains information on 182 courier deliveries.

Courier	Pickup Time	Delivery Time	Mileage	Cost
1	13	14	7	16.55
3	20	51	20	26.50
2	22	33	12	19.00
3	11	47	19	25.60
3	17	18	8	15.70
⋮	⋮	⋮	⋮	⋮

The variables are defined as follows:

Courier: 1 = DFW Express,
               2 = Carborne Carrier,
               3 = Metro Delivery.

Pickup Time: Time in minutes from when the order is phoned in until a courier agent arrives.

Delivery Time: Time in minutes that it takes for the documents to be delivered to the destination from the firm.

Mileage: Distance in miles from the law firm to the destination.

Cost: Charge for the delivery. Each of the courier services charges a flat fee plus a mileage charge. These charges vary from courier to courier.

Case Questions: Fastest Courier in the West

Name _____

1. Based on your analysis, which of the three courier services would you recommend to the law firm? Why?

2. Which variable (or variables) did you use as the main criterion for making your decision? Explain why.

3. Which statistical tools did you use to *summarize* the data? Attach any relevant output.

4. Which statistical inference method(s) is most useful for comparing the courier services? Describe the results of this analysis.

5. Give a brief outline of the steps you took in your data analysis. Point to specific discoveries that you made during your analysis which suggested what to do next and eventually led to your conclusions and recommendation. Attach a copy of any relevant output.

Direct Discount Linens

Roger and Mary McConnell received venture funding to begin a new direct marketing business in Creve Coeur, a fast growing suburb of St. Louis. Like many entrepreneurs, the McConnells have come to believe that consumers are becoming continually more comfortable with making purchases over the phone and through catalogs, thus avoiding inconvenient, timely, and frustrating trips to the store. Their new business would be aimed at this direct marketing segment.

The McConnells plan to sell top-of-the-line linen products that are commonly used in bedrooms and dining rooms (*e.g.*, sheets, pillow cases, table cloths and napkins). These products have traditionally been sold in specialty and department stores. Overhead costs for such stores, however, are often considerable, given the need to locate them in or near large shopping malls. By using a catalog instead of a retail store, the McConnells will enjoy a considerable cost advantage. Their business plan calls for passing on a large portion of the overhead cost savings to consumers by providing high quality merchandise at deep discounts.

As an early step in implementing their business plan, the McConnells put together an expensive sales brochure, containing high quality, large color photographs of their merchandise. This catalog would be mailed to a market segment specifically chosen to reflect the demographic mix of people who make linen purchases in department and up-scale specialty stores. The initial mailing list contained the names of over 4,000 high potential customers in the greater St. Louis area.

Like all entrepreneurs, the McConnells wanted to get their new business off to a good start. They were convinced that the typical consumer of high quality linen products is fully aware of brand names, and thus would be willing to purchase this type of merchandise through direct marketing. They were also convinced that once consumers gave their direct marketing service a try, they would find that the quality of their products and service, in addition to the discounted prices, would keep them as repeat customers. Nonetheless, like so many direct marketers, the McConnells were worried that this relatively expensive sales catalog would not receive consumers' attention and/or would get misplaced or thrown out before consumers were ready to purchase linen products. Thus, the McConnells wanted to use a sales promotion that would encourage new customers to pay attention to and use their catalog.

The McConnells' business plan included a one month trial period in which they could experiment with different sales promotion techniques designed to encourage potential consumers to buy from their catalog. In particular, they decided to include a discount coupon with each catalog in order to encourage consumers to use them. Each coupon would be good for a percentage discount off their initial purchase from the catalog. However, the McConnells had no idea about how large the discount should be to encourage such purchases. They wanted it to be large enough to bring in sales, but not so large that they failed to make a good profit.

They decided to conduct a marketing experiment using three different discount levels: 10% off, 15% off, and 20% off. For this purpose, they randomly selected 50 consumers from their mailing list to receive each of these three discount coupons. The McConnells also sent out fifty catalogs to consumers without any coupon in order to check on whether or not it was necessary to use discount coupons at all. Discount coupons had to be used within 15 days from their receipt.

The McConnells hoped that the results of their consumer experiment would help them decide among these discount coupon choices as they prepared to launch their new business. Thus, a total of 200 catalogs were distributed to randomly selected potential customers, 50 persons in each discount group and another 50 persons who received no discount coupon at all.

In order to understand the impact of the discount coupons, the wholesale cost of the merchandise and the costs of doing business need to be considered. The costs associated with producing and distributing sales catalogs ($9.00 per catalog distributed to each of the 200 prospective customers) reflect costs to Direct Discount Linens. Sales tax on each transaction as well as shipping and handling charges represent costs to the customer.

Data were collected regarding: (a) whether or not the household received a coupon, and if so, the size discount that was offered, (b) whether or not a purchase had been made, and (c) the retail dollar amount of that transaction, the wholesale cost of the merchandise ordered, and the fixed and variable transaction costs for that sale.

Assignment

The collected data are located in the DDLINENS.DAT file on the Data Disk. The Data Description section contains the structure of this data file. Inspect the data in DDLINENS.DAT and assist the McConnells in developing an implementation plan for their direct marketing company. In particular, determine whether or not receiving a coupon makes a difference in consumer purchase behavior. If receiving a coupon does make a difference, what size coupon would you recommend to the McConnells? Use your analysis of the data in DDLINENS.DAT to support your recommendations.

Data Description

The file DDLINENS.DAT on the Data Disk contains information on each actual sales transaction made during the 15-day testing period. Data for all consumers who made a purchase are recorded in the manner depicted below.

Retail Price	Discount	Retail After Discount	Sales Tax	S&H	Purchase Total	Cost of Goods	Catalog Cost per Purchase
33.59	0	33.59	2.35	4.03	39.97	17.44	25.00
43.43	0	43.43	3.04	4.59	51.06	24.84	25.00
112.48	10	101.23	7.09	8.47	116.79	64.07	13.64
90.62	10	81.56	5.71	7.23	94.50	56.49	13.64
85.80	15	72.93	5.11	6.94	84.98	50.37	13.24
72.23	15	61.40	4.30	6.18	71.88	43.79	13.24
67.75	20	54.20	3.79	5.91	63.90	38.68	11.25
66.12	20	52.90	3.70	5.82	62.42	38.49	11.25
⋮	⋮	⋮	⋮	⋮	⋮	⋮	⋮

These data are coded as follows:

Retail Price: Retail price of merchandise purchased.

Discount: Size of coupon discount: 0, 10, 15, or 20%.

Retail After Discount: Retail price of the merchandise after discount.

Sales Tax: Sales tax paid by the customer which is 7% of the retail price of the merchandise after discount.

S&H: Shipping and handling charges paid by the customer.

Purchase Total: Total cost of purchase paid by the
                                   customer (Retail After Discount minus
                                   Sales Tax and Shipping and Handling).

Cost of Goods: Wholesale cost of the purchased
                                   merchandise to Direct Discount Linens.

Catalog Cost per Purchase: The cost of developing and shipping
                                   catalogs is $9.00 for each catalog sent to
                                   a potential customer. This cost is
                                   expressed per purchase within each group
                                   of 50 persons in the marketing
                                   experiment. The per purchase cost
                                   reflects $450.00 (per group) divided by
                                   the total number of purchases made
                                   within that group.

Case Questions: Direct Discount Linens

Name _____

1. Does receiving a coupon make a difference in consumer purchase behavior? (Circle one)

    YES   NO

    What data did you consider in answering this question?

    What evidence leads you to this conclusion?

2. What size coupon would you recommend the McConnells use? (Circle one.)

0%   10%   15%   20%

What data did you consider in answering this question?

What evidence leads you to this conclusion?

Avalon Cosmetics, Inc.

"Ladies and gentleman, I think we've got a problem that requires some clear thinking and sound decisions, if we're going to be in business two years from now." That's how Carol Sanderson began the emergency meeting she called of her planning committee. Ms. Sanderson is the founder and CEO of Avalon Cosmetics, a regional, full-line cosmetics company headquartered in Chicago.

Avalon Cosmetics was founded almost two decades ago as a copy-cat version of Avon and Mary Kay, two highly successful door-to-door cosmetics companies. Sales associates, called "beauty consultants," knock on doors in their territories and offer housewives free make-overs in hopes of selling cosmetics and grooming supplies.

The Avalon "work force" is made up of women who act as independent contractors to the company. They typically are married and have one or more school-age children. If they are aggressive, they can make a good living with Avalon. As importantly, because they have control over their work schedules, they can fit their work in with their family and social obligations.

Avalon has a very high profit margin, in part because it has a relatively low overhead burden. Beauty consultants must buy their sample kits and inventory, process and deliver all merchandise, and service customer complaints — all in exchange for a percentage of their sales. Thus, Avalon pays relatively few fixed costs. Avalon does, however, have a high opportunity cost if a territory does not produce expected revenues. Nancy

Mackay, Avalon's Director of Marketing, has clarified repeatedly that women will spend money on cosmetics. As she often notes, "If the customers don't spend their money on our products, they will spend it on a competitor's products!" It is this clear understanding of the cosmetics market that has Carol Sanderson so concerned. She has seen her company's revenues fall nearly five percent in each of the past two years, and so far, this year looks worse than last! Carol has assembled the planning committee, comprised of the directors of Marketing, Product Development and Human Resources, to focus on this problem and help turn the business around. She has asked them to share their views of the problem and make suggestions for what needs to be done next.

Bill Lamb, Director of Product Development, said he's confused about what to do. He surveyed a sample of customers about their satisfaction with their purchases and said he saw no evidence of a problem. As Bill put it, "We're doing our job — our customers love our products. They say they are repeat customers. They say our prices are right. They say they recommend our products to their friends. They love the personal attention they get from our beauty consultants. I just don't understand why we're getting deeper and deeper in trouble with a such a positive and loyal customer base!"

Nancy Mackay agreed. "We've asked a number of consumer panels about what new products they'd like to see and what modifications are needed in our existing product line. The feedback I get is consistent — we're making what they want to buy. Perhaps we should reconsider our pricing structure, or come up with discounts, or maybe a game — a gimmick — to recapture attention in the market place. We might even need to consider advertising. I know all these suggestions cost money, real money, but if our product line is complete and our products are good, then it seems to me that the only thing left to do is to stir up some interest in our products."

Carol Sanderson liked the idea of an ad campaign, although she dreaded the thought of the costs that would be involved. To reach their target customer base, housewives, they would probably have to advertise on day-time television, during game programs and soap operas. The costs of advertising at that time and for those TV programs, however, might be prohibitive.

Carol continued the discussion by asking, "How else can we reach our customers? We know a lot about our customer base — they're women between the ages of 27 and 44, they stay at home to raise their kids, and they love the attention provided by our beauty consultants."

Cathy Eller, Director of Human Resources, followed up on Carol Sanderson's last comment. Cathy began her comments by asking about how long ago the customer profile was developed. She then said, "The reason I ask is, well, I've been reading a lot lately about the changing demographics of the working world. One magazine article I read pointed out that more and more women are entering the work force. Let's assume this is true — maybe our problem is not the product line, or our pricing, or our advertising. Maybe, our sales are going down because our 'customer' is no longer at home to answer the door when our beauty consultants knock on it! Maybe, just maybe, our customers are among the women who are finding their way into the work force."

This was clearly a very provocative statement. Nobody had considered this possibility. If Cathy's ideas were valid, then it would require some serious thought about what to do. After all, Avalon Cosmetics became successful in part because they were good at developing excellent products at attractive prices and serving their customers with a personal touch. If the problem were not one of product, pricing, or sales approach, they would have to "create" a novel solution that went beyond the assembled expertise of the planning committee.

Carol Sanderson asked, "How do we find out if you're right about this, Cathy?" Do we have access to any information that would be useful?"

Cathy Eller thought for a moment and, with a big smile on her face, announced, "I think we can do it from the information our beauty consultants keep on each of their clients. If you'll remember, beauty consultants are asked to keep information about each client who makes a purchase. They are supposed to record the type of product purchased and the total purchase price of each transaction. We even asked them to record the number of times they called on each customer at home before making a sale and the time of day this customer contact was made. More importantly, we asked them three years ago to get more information about each customer. We asked them for their clients' ages and the number of children each has. I think we even asked them to include information about whether the client had a job outside the home!"

"Great," said Carol Sanderson. "When can we get a summary of that information?"

Cathy responded, "I'll have my staff pull those numbers together and summarize them by our next meeting. I'll even ask them to speculate on what these results might mean for our business. I've got some really bright people working for me who are good at figuring out what needs to be done to solve problems. Who knows, maybe we can turn our problem into an opportunity."

Carol Sanderson agreed that Cathy's staff should "pull together" the numbers, analyze them and interpret the results, and make suggestions about their meaning for the company. She ended the meeting by expressing her hope that Cathy's efforts would lead to somewhere productive.

Cathy Eller went to her customer data base and drew three random samples of 100 customers each who purchased Avalon products during the summers of 1990, 1991 and 1992. She had her staff contact the beauty consultants to obtain relevant information on each of their customers. For each customer, information was collected on: (1) the date of purchase, (2) the amount of purchase, (3) the number of times the beauty consultant visited a customer's home before making contact with the customer, (4) the time of day that the initial contact was made, (5) the client's age, (6) the number of minor children at home, and (7) whether or not the customer was employed outside the home. These data were coded, and a computer file was created in preparation for data analysis.

Assignment

As a member of Cathy Eller's staff, you have been assigned the task of analyzing and interpreting the data that Cathy Eller created. You'll find these data in the AVALON.DAT file on the Data Disk. A description of this data set is given in the Data Description section. Your analyses should be aimed at comparing the descriptions of customers over the past three years. Once you have completed your statistical analyses and have interpreted those findings, you are to make suggestions to Cathy Eller about the business directions suggested by the data. You will need to be creative in deciding what these data might mean about the continued success of Avalon Cosmetics. The Case Questions will guide your thinking on this assignment. Use important details from your analysis to support your recommendations.

Data Description

The AVALON.DAT file on the Data Disk contains information on 300 Avalon Cosmetics customers from the summers of 1990, 1991 and 1992. Data are grouped by year. (See the Important Note below.)

Year	Month	Day	Purchase Price	Number of Contacts	Time of Day	Employed	Age	Number of Children
90	6	15	3.53	1	1	0	35	2
90	6	17	10.99	3	3	1	36	0
⋮	⋮	⋮	⋮	⋮	⋮	⋮	⋮	⋮
91	6	8	8.57	2	1	0	36	4
91	6	4	12.23	2	1	0	39	0
⋮	⋮	⋮	⋮	⋮	⋮	⋮	⋮	⋮
92	6	10	19.25	1	1	0	41	2
92	8	20	14.22	3	3	1	39	0
⋮	⋮	⋮	⋮	⋮	⋮	⋮	⋮	⋮

The variables are defined as follows:

Year: Year in which the purchase was made.

Month: Month in which the purchase was made.

Day: Date on which the purchase was made.

Purchase Price: Retail price of merchandise purchased.

Number of Contacts: Number of times the sales associate visited the home before making contact with the customer.

Time of Day: Time of day when initial contact was made (1 = morning, 2 = afternoon, and 3 = evening).

Employed: 1, if customer is employed outside the home, 0, otherwise.

Age: The customer's age in years.

Number of Children: The number of minor children at home.

IMPORTANT NOTE: Due to the size of the data file AVALON.DAT, some student versions of statistical software packages may not be capable of analyzing this data set. Consult your instructor if you have any problems.

Case Questions: Avalon Cosmetics, Inc.

Name _____

1. Compute descriptive statistics, and prepare tables and/or graphs, for all relevant variables in the data set. Separate analyses need to be conducted for each yearly sample. Note that some variables are continuous variables while others are discrete.

2. Prepare tables that summarize the results of your analyses across the three-year period. Are the yearly samples different from each other? Explain.

3. Do these findings suggest that Carol Sanderson's description of the typical customer is correct? Explain.

4. Based on your analysis, write your description of the typical customer in 1992.

5. Would Nancy Mackay's suggestion of advertising during daytime TV shows be a cost-effective solution to Avalon's business problems? Explain why or why not.

6. Based on your description of the typical customer in 1992, make one or more recommendations for refocusing how Avalon Cosmetics conducts its business to insure its success into the near future.

Devon College

Devon College has always enjoyed a wonderful reputation for providing a liberal arts education, and recently Devon has been recognized as one of the top 25 educational values in the country among private universities. Alumni are frequently quoted on how positive their experiences were while on campus. Indeed, Devon has established a track record for graduating students who are in demand. It places its graduates in some of the nation's finest professional and graduate schools and in some of America's top companies.

Devon College is located in a rural community in upper New England. It is a small, liberal arts institution with an enrollment of just over 2,000 students. While it draws 80 percent of its student body from the New England area, it attracts students from throughout the country as well. Devon's faculty and administrators agree that exposure to diversity is an important component of a liberal education and encourage it in many forms, to include geographical diversity. In fact, Devon's advertising literature proudly states that its students come from over 25 states and from dozens of countries from around the world.

Despite its reputation, Devon College, like all four year undergraduate institutions, has fallen on increasingly hard times. The demand for higher education has fallen due to the drop in college-aged students, the increased costs for providing education has risen due to inflation, and donations and other gifts have fallen due to the depressed economy during the past several years. While these trends do not project disaster for the college in either the near or long term, the Chancellor of Devon College, Bill Stevens, has asked each unit on campus to examine its expenditures and insure that college monies are being spent wisely.

Angela Brock, Director of Admissions, has called her staff together to begin this process. Brock's operation is responsible for recruiting new students to campus and then orienting entering freshmen once they arrive. The admission's office divides its staff time, and resources, among several key responsibilities — providing tours to prospective students who visit campus, visiting other cities across the nation on recruiting trips, providing information as requested on Devon's "1–800" recruiting number, sending information packets to prospective students who request it, and running the annual campus orientation program for incoming freshmen.

A full 30 percent of Brock's budget goes to making recruiting visits to other campuses. Of this budget, approximately 50 percent is spent visiting campuses in cities and states in the New England region. The rest of the money is spent on visits to major cities in the Midwest, West, Southwest and South. It is these visits that Brock has called her staff together to discuss.

Angela Brock began the meeting by stating, "Bill Stevens has asked all units on campus to examine their expenditures and be sure that they actually contribute to the unit's mission. I've taken a look at our budget and think that we're OK on the orientation programs, information services and campus tours. I'm not so sure about our recruitment tour program. Given its expense, I feel that maybe it's time we examine this program and make some judgment about its effectiveness. Any thoughts?"

Bernie Shyna was the first to speak. He said, "I think we need to cut out all trips to the West Coast, particularly LA and San Francisco. Those kids don't really seem to fit in here. I mean, they're over 2,000 miles from home and in what has to be a strange part of the world to them. We can save over ten thousand dollars a year just by cutting out those two cities alone!"

Mary Washington agreed and added that kids from any other region of the country have a hard time adjusting not only socially, but academically as well. She said her sister roomed with a girl from San Francisco who dropped out after the first semester and that she knew of two other girls from the West Coast who dropped out after the first year.

Kara Roberts, however, disagreed. As Kara put it, "I think we might be jumping the gun here. I also know students whom we recruited from the West Coast, and they did great! If we simply rely on what we happen to hear, we might be making a big mistake in evaluating these recruiting trips. It seems to me that we can answer questions about whether it's useful to visit cities like LA by actually seeing what has occurred to the all students, as a group, that we've recruited from these cities. Maybe Todd and Mary are right — but maybe not. I'd be willing to look at the data and report back to the committee."

Mary Washington didn't hesitate to agree with Kara. She said she may have been too hasty in passing on what she'd heard about some of the girls and offered to help. In fact, everybody at the table thought that Kara had a good idea and several offered to help. That's when Kara asked, "Exactly what kind of information will it take to suggest that we should stop going to a particular city?" This brought another round of discussion, with a number of people making useful suggestions.

Angela Brock summarized the ideas by stating, "We'll take a look at the recruiting efforts for selected cities in different parts of the country. I suggest we focus on our most expensive recruiting trips. That would be Los Angeles and San Francisco in the West, Houston in the Southwest, Chicago in the Midwest and Atlanta and Miami in the South. Each of these trips have budgets around $10,000. We'll examine data for all students who enrolled as freshmen in each of the past couple of years. We'll create a data file that contains information about those recruiting efforts from our admission and enrollment records. Kay Freeman and Bernie Shyna will put this together for us. We should be able to identify the students who came to Devon as freshmen, and of those students, the ones who dropped out during their first year and the ones who completed their first year. Can you think of anything else we should consider?"

Bernie added that they also should look at the number of persons who received admission offers but didn't come to Devon. The group thought that was a good idea. Kara suggested that they also look at the "demographics" of those who were successful. Everyone seemed to like this idea as well. She also thought that it would be interesting to see how many students graduated from those who started as freshmen, but that idea wasn't as well received.

Angela didn't want to wait to see how many students in their yearly samples would actually graduate in the next four to five years. Instead, she suggested an alternative, proxy measure. She said, "We have pretty good results from other institutional research studies that can help us estimate eventual graduation rates. In fact, our own studies indicate that approximately 85 percent of the students who survive their first year of college with a GPA of 2.50 or higher will graduate within five years of entering Devon. Of those who complete their first year with a lower GPA, about sixty percent fail to graduate. These data make it pretty clear that ..."

Kara interrupted Angela and, excitedly, said, "Well, if that's the case, then we might want to project graduation rates from the GPA's of students who finish their first year. I know that this won't be perfect, but maybe this will help us decide whether it's a good idea, for Devon and for the students, to continue to recruit from a particular city."

Again, everyone agreed. Angela added GPA to the list and asked for additional sources of information. After a brief discussion that failed to add additional ideas, Angela asked Kay and Bernie to gather the information from the recruitment and registrar's records and enter them on a diskette so that they might be examined. She then asked Kara if she needed any help in analyzing, interpreting, and writing up the results for each of the cities they would select. Kara said that she would appreciate any help that Angela might be able to provide.

Assignment

You have been asked to help Kara Roberts analyze and interpret the data and write a report summarizing the efforts to decide which cities should be dropped from the recruiting itinerary. The data, collected by Kay and Bernie, are contained in the DEVON.DAT file on the Data Disk. This file provides information on persons who were recruited in each of six specific cities from throughout the United States. Data were collected for the last two recruiting classes for which entering students had the opportunity to complete their freshmen year. In total, data were collected for 209 entering freshmen across this two year period. In addition, data were collected for a group of 87 prospective students who were offered admission but chose to

go to school elsewhere. For all persons in the data base, information was collected on race and gender. Since 96 percent of the students were between 18 and 19 years of age, this information was not recorded. For those who actually enrolled at Devon, information concerning whether or not they completed their freshmen year and the GPA's of those who did so were also recorded. A complete description of this data file is contained in the Data Description section.

You have been assigned to help Kara Roberts with this project. Your analysis should be aimed at examining the data in each of the six cities for each of the two yearly samples and, based on your interpretation of the findings, identifying those cities for which recruiting should and should not be continued. The Case Questions will guide your thinking. Use important details from your analysis to support your recommendation.

Data Description

The DEVON.DAT file on the Data Disk contains information on 296 prospective students, 209 of whom actually enrolled as a freshman at Devon College. All potential students were recruited from six cities over a two year period. Data are grouped together by city. A partial listing of the data is shown below. A "*" indicates non-response or missing information. (See the Important Note below.)

YEAR	CITY	ENROLLED	GENDER	RACE	STAYED	GPA
90	1	1	1	1	1	3.70
90	1	1	1	1	1	2.42
90	1	1	1	1	1	2.75
90	1	1	2	1	1	1.90
90	1	1	2	2	1	2.27
90	1	1	1	1	1	3.23
⋮	⋮	⋮	⋮	⋮	⋮	⋮

These data are coded as follows:

YEAR: 1 = in first year recruitment sample,
                 2 = in second year recruitment sample.

CITY: 1 = Los Angeles,
                 2 = San Francisco,
                 3 = Houston,
                 4 = Chicago,
                 5 = Miami,
                 6 = Atlanta.

ENROLLED: 1 = actually enrolled at Devon,
                 0 = did not enroll at Devon.

GENDER: 1 = female,
                 2 = male.

RACE: 1 = non-minority,
                 2 = minority.

STAYED: 1 = completed freshman year,
                 0 = did not complete freshman year.

GPA: Grade point average at the end of the freshman year
                 (A = 4, B = 3, C = 2, D = 1, F = 0).

IMPORTANT NOTE: The symbol "*" (asterisk) is used in the data file DEVON.DAT to denote non-response or missing data. Consult your statistical software documentation for a list of valid missing data codes. If your statistical software package does not accept "*" as a valid missing code, you have two options. Your statistical software package may allow you to specify another missing code. Otherwise, you will need to change each occurrence of "*" in the data file to a missing symbol that is acceptable to your particular statistics package. This can be done by editing the file DEVON.DAT within a word processing package. See your instructor if you need assistance.

Case Questions: Devon College

Name _____

1. Compute descriptive statistics, and prepare tables and/or graphs, for all relevant variables in the data set. Separate analyses need to be conducted for each yearly sample. Note that some variables are continuous and others are discrete.

2. Are the yearly samples different from each other on any variable? Explain. What findings lead you to this conclusion?

3. Do the cities differ in terms of the percentage of persons who receive offers and actually enroll as freshmen? If so, how do the cities differ? What findings lead you to this conclusion?

4. Do the cities differ in terms of the percentage of freshmen who finish their first year of study? If so, how do the cities differ? What findings lead you to this conclusion?

5. Do the cities differ in terms of the GPA's of students who finish their first year of study? If so, how do the cities differ? What findings lead you to this conclusion?

6. Do the cities differ in terms of the likelihood of graduation after four/five years of college? If so, how do the cities differ? What findings lead you to this conclusion?

7. Based on your findings, make recommendations regarding which cities should be dropped from the recruiting efforts. At approximately $10,000 per city, how much money can be saved without having an impact on Devon's recruitment mission?

8. How confident are you of your recommendations? Explain.

Checker's Pizza

Checker's Pizza is a chain of 40 pizza restaurants in the New England area. Checker's started in 1975 and specialized in making pizzas "from scratch." Each pizza was covered with a special sauce, made from a "secret" family recipe, that kept customers coming back for more. But Checker's, like other pizza restaurants in the 80's, had to respond to the wave of fast food pizza restaurants and delivery services that seemed to corner the market.

Checker's responded to this threat by changing the way they did business. Not only did they expand their product line and start delivering pizzas like their competitors, they also started making pizza using the same "fast food" procedures as their competitors. Old customers were acutely aware that the pizzas were different. But, while the pizzas are now made using a conveyer oven from dough that is made in a central kitchen, frozen and then delivered to each restaurant, the sauce had not changed at all. And that was the key to their growth. While old customers knew that the pizzas were not as good, new customers only knew that they were better pizzas than Checker's competitors made.

Even still, the pizza business had fallen on hard times by the late 80's. Competition for customers in the fast food business had soared and the weak economy at that time had slowed business for everybody. It was in this business climate that Terri Chester was hired as General Manager of the Checker's Pizza chain. She joined the company almost two years ago. Her job was to restore the market share and profit of this business.

Terri attempted to address her mission in a systematic fashion. She worked with her executive team to identify and prioritize key issues, and then set up a series of task forces to deal with those problems that required immediate attention. Among the key problems identified was one associated with employee turnover. The turnover rate for store personnel was considered extremely high. Terri knew that such a high turnover rate not only impacted expenses due to costs of replacing persons who quit, but also impacted customer service as well. It's hard to serve customers well with a continual flow of recently hired staff who have yet to fully learn their jobs.

Checker's Pizza, like all fast food restaurants, employs teenagers in most positions. They work as counter persons, wait staff, cooks, and delivery persons. As is typical with this employee population, turnover tends to be high. In the fast food industry, restaurant turnover for younger employees typically ranges from 200 to 600 percent per year! Given such high turnover rates in this industry, replacement costs can add up to a considerable sum. These costs reflect dollars actually spent on recruitment, interviewing, hiring and training, as well as non-tangible costs associated with having staff who haven't climbed the learning curve to fully pull their own weight on the job. The employee turnover task force estimated that it costs Checker's approximately $250 to replace someone who quits.

Over the past three years, turnover at Checker's Pizza has occurred at an average annual rate of 350 percent across all of its restaurants. This translates into newly hired store personnel who stay, on average, approximately 90 days before terminating. Thus, every time someone leaves, the position is refilled by a new employee who, on average, will stay only 90 days. This, in turn, means that on average each store replaces 48 employees over the course of a year since each store has twelve employees. Each time someone leaves, Checker's incurs the costs of recruiting, hiring, training, and developing his or her replacement. At a $250 replacement cost, this adds up to $12,000 in annual replacement costs per store and $480,000 per year across the restaurant chain!

Terri Chester hired a consultant, Dr. Shannon Train, from a local university to conduct a study to try to identify why people were leaving. The consultant contacted a sample of former employees and conducted a brief telephone interview with each. While a large list of specific reasons were identified, the one theme that recurred was the treatment employees received from store management. Leavers said they were often treated "like children" by their managers. Store managers reacted quickly and harshly whenever employees did anything that did not reflect store policy, even for newly hired persons who had yet to fully understand what store policy actually meant. Further, they seldom involved staff in any discussion about problems.

Dr. Train suggested that Terri focus her efforts on store management's treatment of staff, particularly newly hired staff. He said there are a number of approaches commonly used to deal with this problem, and recommended two in particular. First, he suggested that store managers receive a two-day human relations training program designed to not only impress upon them the importance of considering interpersonal relations, but to help managers develop important interpersonal skills that will facilitate good working relationships. The second alternative that Dr. Train recommended was to give store managers an incentive for keeping staff from quitting. He had heard that other companies in the fast food industry have used this approach with some success. He suggested that managers be given $100 (40% of the replacement costs that would have been spent) for keeping employees twice as long than they currently stay employed. Thus, store managers would receive a $100 bonus for each new hire who stayed at least six months (*i.e.*, 180 days). The cost of providing the two-day interpersonal skills workshop would be $500 per manager, or $20,000 for all 40 store managers.

Dr. Train pointed out to Terri that she might want to consider doing both the training and bonus. He noted that a pilot study could help answer the questions without going into the same degree of expense as would be required in a full-scale implementation. As Dr. Train put it:

> If you really hope to put a dent in the retention problem, you might need to both conduct the training and provide the bonus. Think of it this way. To get managers to change their behavior, you need to not only give them a reason to change, but the skills to do so. As I tell my students, empowerment requires enablement. Now, managers may well know exactly how to treat their people to keep them from leaving in droves. If this is true, then you only need to give them some incentive to do so. On the other hand, while your managers may have good interpersonal skills in general, they may not have the needed interpersonal skills to work with teenagers. So, maybe all that's needed is the skills training. It's hard to say, without looking into it more carefully, whether either one or the

other approach will be enough to do the trick or whether both might be necessary.

While Terri Chester liked both ideas, she wasn't ready to proceed simultaneously with both approaches. It would require a substantial commitment of money at a time when money wasn't easy to put into the budget. When she stated her conclusion to Dr. Train, he suggested that Terri run an experiment to see if either, or both, approaches he suggested made an impact on retention before she committed funds company-wide to either approach. That way, she'll know what might work before she commits the funds to both approaches. She liked the idea!

Dr. Train designed an experiment in which 40 store managers were randomly chosen to be in one of four "experimental" conditions that reflected all combinations of the training and bonus conditions: (1) no training-no bonus, (2) no training-bonus, (3) training-no bonus, and (4) training-bonus. Ten store managers were assigned to each condition.

Training and a discussion of the bonus program were done by the end of the month. The actual experiment began the following month. All restaurant staff hired during the month were included in the study. The tenure of each of these persons was followed for 12 months. For each employee in the study, tenure was recorded in days, from the date of hire until the date of termination or until the date the study ended. Thus, tenure could range from one day up to 365 days for those persons who were still employed when the study ended.

Assignment

As of today, all data for this staff retention study have been collected and recorded in computer-ready form. As a member of the retention task force, you have been asked by Terri Chester to examine these data. You'll find the data in CHECKERS.DAT on the Data Disk. A description of this data set is given in the Data Description section.

You are to make a recommendation to Terri Chester regarding whether or not to use either, or both, of the training and bonus interventions to stem the flow of turnover among restaurant staff. The Case Questions will assist you in your analysis of the data. Use important details from your analysis to support your recommendations.

Data Description

The CHECKERS.DAT file on the Data Disk contains the results from the experiment aimed at determining whether the training program and/or the bonus incentive has an effect on employee tenure. Data are recorded in the manner depicted below.

ID	Training	Bonus	Tenure
001	0	0	14
002	0	1	178
003	1	1	164
004	0	1	97
005	1	0	116
⋮	⋮	⋮	⋮

The variables are defined as follows:

ID: Sequential identification numbers assigned to employees included in the study.

Training: 1 = training given to employee's store manager,
0 = no training given.

Bonus: 1 = bonus given to employee's store manager,
0 = no bonus given.

Tenure: Number of days the person was employed, from date of hire to the date of termination or the date the study ended.

Case Questions: Checker's Pizza

Name _____

1. Does either the training or the bonus program or both relate to employee retention? Explain your answer. Attach any supporting data analysis.

2. Draw a graph depicting the effect of the training and bonus programs on employee tenure. Explain, in words, the nature of the relationship you observed.

3. Make a specific recommendation to Terri Chester regarding the use of the training and bonus programs.

ServPro, Inc.

It all started out peaceably enough. Tom Johnson, one of the new service reps, asked Al Washington and Michael Post about their salaries. It was an innocent enough question and the answers suggested that all three were making about the same money. Nobody seemed concerned. Then, Michael Post said that he had seen a memo on his boss' desk on which salaries for the entire department were listed and noticed something "funny." All three of them were near the bottom of the list. In fact, he said, "Just about every other black in the department was in the bottom half of the list."

Well, this started the three of them wondering out loud about whether their company, ServPro, Inc., was discriminating against minorities. They kicked it around all through lunch and then talked about it again each day for the next week. And each day, somebody would come in with information from one of the other offices from throughout the country that continued to suggest that all minorities, not just black employees, were not being paid on par with their white counterparts. They had "rough" information from four additional offices that, when they calculated averages, suggested that minorities were making about $250 a month less than white employees.

This incensed Tom Johnson. He told the others, "When Al Miller recruited me here last year, he told me that ServPro's management believed in affirmative action. He promised me that I would go as far in this company as my effort and good work would take me. I'm not saying that this past year has been bad, but this salary stuff makes me wonder about whether I should stay or start looking for a place where minorities are treated the same as whites!" Al and Michael agreed.

The more they talked, the more they felt betrayed by a company that at first looked like a place that would ignore skin color. Indeed, they were all impressed with the company's strong affirmative action stance. They were told that advancement, and salary, would depend on how well they did their jobs — that they could expect to move from an Assistant Service Rep (Grade 1) to Service Rep (Grade 2) in two to three years and then move to Senior Service Rep (Grade 3) somewhere from three to four years later. They were led to expect annual performance reviews, with pay raises determined by their performance during the previous year. They liked the developmental program ServPro had to offer and looked forward to the responsibility that their jobs would offer as they moved up the career progression ladder. It was disappointing to think that ServPro might turn out to be the kind of place where skin color would limit their opportunities.

Tom Johnson didn't say anything for several weeks about the salary incident. On his own, however, he started reading about fair employment law and his options if he believed that his civil liberties were being violated. He even called the local office of the Equal Employment Opportunity Commission (EEOC) and spoke with a field agent about his situation. The agent, Mr. Mark Malone, suggested that he bring the matter up with his supervisor. Malone told him that, in his experience, appearances were not always what they seemed, and that usually matters such as this are easily explained by the company. He did, however, clarify that a $250 per month salary difference between minorities and non-minorities was not trivial and would, indeed, command the attention of EEOC if Mr. Johnson were still concerned with this issue after going through official company channels.

Tom Johnson, escorted by his two friends, went to see Howard Kirk, his department manager. Kirk seemed somewhat agitated when Johnson confronted him with the "facts." He simply dismissed their protest as complete nonsense. He told the three of them to leave the management work to managers and to get back to work so they could learn their jobs well enough to earn a good evaluation and, thus, a good pay raise next year. When Tom Johnson "wondered out loud" about whether their performance evaluations were chosen to justify lowered pay raises to minorities, Kirk flew off the handle. He abruptly told them to quit trying to cause trouble. He informed them, rather curtly and very loudly, that "... salary is based on performance and loyalty to the company. The single best way you can improve your salaries is to pay as much attention to your jobs as apparently you're paying to information that is none of your business." He then "dismissed" them.

Predictably, Mr. Johnson found the content and tone of Mr. Kirk's remarks offensive. Together with Al Washington and Michael Post, they have now organized a small group of minority peers who have threatened to visit the EEOC claims office in order to pursue their conviction that ServPro practices discriminatory pay practices.

Larry Greer, President of ServPro, got word of the problem almost immediately through the grapevine. Greer called a meeting with Johnson, Washington and Post that afternoon. It was a more relaxed conversation. Greer began by asking them to explain their concerns. Tom Johnson went through the "facts," this time adding information about how they were treated by Howard Kirk.

Greer responded by assuring the three of them that ServPro did not discriminate against anybody. He repeated Mr. Kirk's message about how pay is determined, but without the offensive tone. Indeed, Mr. Greer outlined the voluntary affirmative action program initiated by ServPro over two years ago as being just an example of the philosophy that ServPro values what people do on the job over their race or gender. Mr. Johnson was willing to listen to the pay policy and talk about the affirmative hiring program, but continued to focus on the apparent salary differences that occurred despite such policies. He insisted that salary equity be achieved and, thus, would not relinquish his claim of discrimination. However, because he was impressed by Mr. Greer's statements regarding the company's affirmative stance in hiring, Mr. Johnson expressed a willingness to meet with Greer again, once additional information became available.

Greer promised that he would report back to his three employees personally at the second meeting, based on having looked into this matter and into the data relevant to it. Mr. Johnson, and the others, seemed willing for Mr. Greer to gather and organize that information.

Assignment

You have been appointed to a task force to investigate this discrimination claim. Mr. Greer has a series of issues that your committee must resolve. He has given you access to the employment and pay histories for service reps. These data are contained in the SERVPRO.DAT file on the Data Disk and are described in the Data Description section. You will need to examine the employment and pay history data contained in this file and attempt to resolve the issues brought forth by Mr. Johnson.

Based on your understanding of the issues and your interpretation of the employment and salary data, write a brief report to Mr. Greer summarizing your beliefs about ServPro's liability. The attached Case Questions will guide your thinking. Use important details from your analysis to support your recommendation.

Data Description

The SERVPRO.DAT file on the Data Disk contains the employment and salary data for ServPro's 140 employees. A partial listing of the data is shown below.

ID	Pay Grade	Gender	Race	Married	Age	Tenure	Rating	Salary
1	1	2	2	0	18	0.5	2	890
2	1	2	1	0	25	2.4	3	1360
3	2	2	1	0	23	3.6	7	2070
4	1	1	2	0	26	1.9	3	1190
5	2	2	1	1	22	3.4	6	1290
⋮	⋮	⋮	⋮	⋮	⋮	⋮	⋮	⋮

These data are coded as follows:

ID Number: Sequential ID number assigned to all employees.

Pay Grade: Pay grade (= 1, 2, or 3).

Gender: 1, if female,
2, if male.

Race: 1, if white,
2, if minority.

Married: 1, if married,
0, if non-married.

Age: Age in years at last birthday.

Tenure: Number of years employed as a service representative at ServPro.

Rating: Employee performance rating, on a 10-point scale, where 1 = poor performance and 10 = excellent performance.

Salary: Currently monthly salary, expressed in dollars.

Case Questions: ServPro, Inc.

Name _____

1. What is the difference between the average salary of minorities and non-minorities? Does this evidence support Mr. Johnson's claim of discrimination?

2. What proportion of minority and non-minority employees are found in each pay grade? How do these proportions influence Mr. Johnson's claim of salary discrimination? Do these proportional differences suggest discrimination in promotions across racial groups?

3. What is the average tenure of minority and non-minority employees in each pay grade? Do these results suggest discrimination in promotions across racial groups?

4. When was the company's Affirmative Action program started? Does this information help explain why more minorities are in the lower pay grades? Explain.

5. What data should be examined to see whether ServPro rewards performance and loyalty, as claimed by Mr. Greer?

6. What type of analyses would indicate if pay was dependent upon performance and loyalty? Do these results suggest that ServPro rewards performance and loyalty? Explain.

7. Do your analyses support Mr. Johnson's allegation of discrimination? Briefly explain why the salary data suggest apparent discrimination and what will "remedy" this salary discrepancy?

Ryder Appraisal District

Ryder Appraisal District (RAD) is the county agency responsible for property taxation in Ryder County, South Carolina. RAD is charged with the appraisal of property for tax purposes, the determination of the amount of tax owed by a property owner, and the collection of these property taxes. There are approximately 12,000 residential properties in Ryder County.

James Bradford was elected last year to the position of Ryder County Tax Commissioner. For many years, taxpayers have complained about the inequities in residential property tax assessments in Ryder County. Bradford promised county residents that, if elected, he would do what he could to make the property taxing system more equitable.

The current residential property taxing system in Ryder County has evolved over several decades. Unimproved property, *i.e.*, a residential lot without a house, is currently taxed at a flat amount of $150. Owners of improved residential property are charged a flat amount plus an additional amount based on the characteristics of the house built on the property, such as the total square footage of heated/cooled floor space, the number of bedrooms, the number of bathrooms, etc. If the owner actually lives in the house, he is given a homestead exemption which reduces his property tax bill by a fixed 10%. If that homeowner is also retired, he is entitled to a retirement exemption that reduces his property tax bill by another 10%. While it would seem that the current system of taxing is fair, several factors have led to inequities.

Each year, new property assessments are mailed out to property owners. These assessments tell the property owners the value of their property as determined by RAD for taxing purposes. After the new assesments are mailed, the property owners are given the opportunity over a period of one month to contest their assessments. A panel known as the County Review Board hears the appeals and makes any adjustments they deem necessary to property assessments. The County Review Board has been known in the past for being "too responsive" in changing assessed values. Those homeowners who complain to the Board are usually granted their reduction. Unfortunately, many of these decisions have led to taxing inconsistencies and discrepancies across the county.

RAD is supposed to reappraise each piece of residential property once every three years. In this way, the RAD data base is kept up to date and includes recent improvements to residential property, such as swimming pools or other additions. However, due to poor economic conditions, county governments have been receiving less and less funding from the state and federal governments. The appraisal staff at RAD has dwindled in the past few years to one full-time appraiser and there are no funds available for hiring professional appraisers on a part-time basis. Over time, the data base has become outdated and inaccurate. This, of course, has led to further inequities in the taxing system.

James Bradford has proposed a simplified property tax assessment plan that he hopes will avoid the problems and inequities of the past and cost less to implement than the current system. His plan is to tax unimproved property in the same way as before using the current rate based on lot size. For improved properties, the new tax will consist of a flat tax plus an amount based on the square footage of heated/cooled space in the house. Both the flat tax and the variable tax components are yet to be determined. Bradford has decided to maintain the current 10% reductions for homestead exemptions and retired homeowners. The square footage measurement would be made once for each house, with an appraisal update occurring whenever an addition is made to the house. This will reduce the workload of RAD appraisers and the amount of necessary recordkeeping. The simplified taxing system should also result in more consistency in taxation and fewer complaints from homeowners about incorrect assessments.

There have been two major concerns expressed about switching to the simplified tax assessment plan. First, it is important to try to keep individual taxes under the new plan as close as possible to what they are currently, otherwise there will be problems. Everyone understands that some property owners will have higher taxes and others will have lower taxes, but the size of the changes should be minimized as much as possible. Secondly, the new tax plan must be revenue-neutral, that is, the total amount of property taxes under the new structure should be roughly the same as before. James Bradford has said that attention to the first concern will largely mitigate this second concern.

The current database contains information on the square footage of each house in Ryder County. Bradford believes that these data may not be accurate. In most cases, the recorded square footage is reported by the builder and is never checked by RAD. Before launching a massive effort to determine the square footage of each house in Ryder County, Bradford has decided to see whether or not the current data are sufficiently accurate.

In fact, James Bradford believes that he can kill two birds with one stone. He has collected a random sample of 80 residential properties from around the county. Over the course of the past two months, the staff appraiser has examined the houses on these properties and their blueprints to come up with an accurate estimate of the actual square footage of heated/cooled space of each house. Other information from the RAD data base was also included in the sample information. From this sample, James Bradford wants to do two things. First, he wants to know whether or not the square footage estimates in the current data base differ significantly from the actual square footage values. Secondly, he wants to use the sample data to estimate the flat tax and the tax rate per square foot that must be charged in order to minimize the changes from the current tax system for improved property owners.

Assignment

The data from the sample of 80 residential properties are contained in the file RYDER.DAT on the Data Disk. The Data Description section contains a description of this data file.

Using this data set and other information given in the case, first help James Bradford decide whether or not the square footage information in the data base is significantly different from the actual values. After that, determine the flat tax amount and the tax charged per square foot that will accomplish his goals. The Case Questions will assist you in your analysis of the data. Use important details from your analysis to support your recommendation.

Data Description

The data for the Ryder Appraisal District case is contained in the file RYDER.DAT on the Data Disk. The file contains information on a sample of 80 residential properties in Ryder County. A partial listing of the data is shown below.

SUB	BLK	LOT	IMP	HSX	RET	REC SQFT	ACT SQFT	TAX
7	3	34	1	1	1	1595	1598	922.48
2	21	47	1	1	1	1855	1876	1047.90
11	8	52	1	1	0	1538	1528	967.03
9	21	8	1	1	0	1687	1713	985.22
2	21	51	1	1	0	1785	1764	1031.35
5	19	66	1	1	1	2084	2107	1093.42
⋮	⋮	⋮	⋮	⋮	⋮	⋮	⋮	⋮

These data are coded as follows:

SUB: Subdivision in which the property is located.

BLOCK: Block in the subdivision in which the property is located.

LOT: Lot number of the property. (SUB, BLOCK, and LOT together describe the location of the property.)

IMP: 1, if improved (*i.e.*, a house is built on the property), 0, if unimproved.

HSX: 1, if homestead exemption (*i.e.*, owner lives in house), 0, otherwise.

RET: 1, if owner retired and HSX = 1, 0, otherwise.

REC SQFT: Square footage recorded in the RAD data base.

ACT SQFT: Actual square footage as measured by RAD appraiser.

TAX: Current county tax on the property under the existing taxing system.

Case Questions: Ryder Appraisal District

Name _____

1. Examine the data for the 80 residential properties using appropriate statistical summaries. Are the data collected on the 80 residential properties suitable for the analysis? If not, describe any adjustments that need to be made.

2. Based on the data collected, are the square footage figures in the RAD data base reasonably accurate? Explain your answer and support your conclusions from the data.

3. Perform an appropriate statistical test to determine if the mean recorded square footage in the entire RAD data base is significantly different from the mean actual square footage for all houses represented in the data base. What recommendation would you make to James Bradford based on your answers to this question and the previous question? Explain.

4. Use an appropriate statistical technique with the data to determine values for the fixed and variable (with respect to square footage) tax components for improved properties in Ryder County. Explain how your approach to estimating these components will meet the concerns of James Bradford about the new tax system being "revenue-neutral" (*i.e.*, keeping property taxes about the same as under the current system, both on an individual property basis and on a total basis).

5. Were there any unusual data that had a large effect on your estimates of the fixed and variable tax components? How did you deal with these influential data in your analysis? Provide the supporting logic behind your approach to dealing with these influential data.

Westmore MBA Program

The MBA program at Westmore University has undergone several dramatic changes over the past five years. During that time, the goal of the business school was to recruit as many students as possible into the MBA program in order to build up their student base and credit hour production. A massive campaign was launched five years ago in order to attract more applicants to the program. Special brochures containing information about the program were printed and mailed to prospective students as well as to other colleges and universities that were likely to have undergraduate students who might be interested in coming to Westmore. Mailings were also sent to students who indicated an interest in Westmore on their GMAT exam. (The GMAT exam is a national standardized test used by most business schools in making admissions decisions for applicants to their graduate programs.) Representatives from the Westmore School of Business began attending regional "MBA fairs," conventions where MBA programs are able to meet with prospective MBA students and share information. In the beginning, the number of students applying to the Westmore MBA program was small, but eventually the advertising campaign began to work and the number of qualified applicants each year increased to the target value of 150 initially set by the dean of the business school and the director of the MBA program. The yield, *i.e.*, the number of admitted applicants who actually enroll and attend Westmore, is typically around 70%. Admitted students who do not enroll either attend other MBA programs or accept job offers. The table below shows the admissions and enrollment figures for the five years of the MBA student base building plan at Westmore.

Year	Admissions	Enrollment
1	86	54
2	108	77
3	134	91
4	141	96
5	154	106

Wayne McDonald, the director of the program, is currently putting the second phase of the plan into action. He knows that in order for the MBA program at Westmore to attain national recognition they must become more selective in the admissions process. The number of applicants is now large enough to do this without falling below a critical mass of 60 enrolled students each year.

The major issue facing Wayne and the MBA program is how to go about selecting students into the program. Wayne recently met with the MBA Admissions Committee which consists of himself and two faculty members, Dr. Susan Thompson, who is a finance professor, and Dr. Hector Gonzalez, who is a marketing professor.

Wayne: "Thanks for coming to the meeting today. As you both know, our recruiting effort over the past five years has been extremely successful. We were able to exceed our original enrollment goal last year. While many of our students have been outstanding and have given our program visibility in the business community, we have had a number of weak performers. Professors have watered down their courses to keep these people afloat in the program. If we are to have a nationally recognized, quality MBA program, we must become stricter in our admission policies. Fortunately, we are now at the point where we can be much more selective and still have our minimum critical mass of 60 enrolled students each year."

Susan: "Wayne is right. Our current admission standards require a minimum score of 400 on the GMAT and a minimum undergraduate grade point average of 2.0. Obviously, this is not much of a hurdle. Personally, I would like to see the minimum requirements set at 580 on the GMAT and 2.75 for the undergraduate grade point average."

Wayne: "Well, raising the minimums is one way of going about it, but there are many other factors that determine the degree of success a student has in our MBA program. We should consider including these factors in our decision making process."

Hector: "Too bad we don't know in advance which students are going to excel. Wayne, do you know what other schools are doing?"

Wayne: "From conferences that I've attended, I have found that many MBA programs put a lot of emphasis on the GMAT score and the undergraduate grade point average of the student. While some schools set minimum entrance requirement on each of these criteria as we do currently, other schools combine these measures into a single overall score. For instance, there is a 'formula score' that many schools use which multiplies the undergraduate GPA by 200 and adds the result to the GMAT score. If the formula score is above a certain figure, say 1000, then the student is considered to be admittable."

Susan: "But there are so many other factors to consider. Surely we don't want our admissions decisions to be based solely on a formula. There are many students who attend colleges with high grade inflation. Those applicants would have an unfair advantage over applicants from stronger schools with regard to undergraduate grade point average."

Hector: "Yes, I agree. There are also studies that have indicated the GMAT is not a strong predictor of success in graduate school for many reasons, including cultural bias."

Wayne: "I am not advocating that we go to a strictly mathematical basis for making our decisions. However, higher minimum standards than we currently have or some sort of formula involving GMAT and undergraduate grade point average might be a useful screening device for sifting through applicants."

Susan: "I'm not opposed to your suggestion. Such an approach could be used to identify those students with high potential for succeeding in our program. In a sense, many of these decisions could be automated."

Wayne: "That would certainly be a great timesaver. Our admissions committee would only have to meet to discuss those applicants with other strong characteristics or extenuating circumstances."

Susan: "Excellent idea! Now, if we go with raising the minimum requirements for GMAT and undergraduate GPA, how much should we raise them? Or if we go with a combined score approach, what formula should we use and how should we set its cutoff values?"

Wayne: "We could go with your earlier suggestion of a 580/2.75 minimum requirement or with the formula score I described earlier. I could talk with directors of other MBA programs to get some feel for how they set their cutoff criteria. After we gain some experience with future admissions, we could adjust the cutoff criteria."

Hector: "Why wait until then? We have five years worth of data already! We should be able to develop our own criteria based on our own past experience."

Susan: "We might even want to consider developing our own formula."

Wayne: "Great ideas! That's why I like working with the two of you on this committee. However, I would limit the data to the last two years because of several changes we made in the program a few years back. The data for the last two years are more reflective of our current program."

Hector: "In looking at these data, how are we going to measure the degree to which a student is successful in our program? Whether they graduate or not?"

Wayne: "Fortunately or unfortunately, depending on how you look at it, practically all of our students have eventually graduated. One of the things we are trying to accomplish is to make our program more rigorous and demanding, to raise the level of quality. If this is going to happen, we have to be more selective with the students we admit."

Susan: "Why not consider the grade point average of the student at the end of the program?"

Wayne: "The major problem there is that the students in our program do not take the same set of courses in their second year because they select different areas of concentration. Some go into marketing, some into finance, others into either accounting or management. There is a real lack of comparability in those final GPA figures. But what we might do is look at the first-year GPA in the MBA program. The courses taken by students in the first year are essentially the same because they are required core courses. It is not until their second year that they began taking elective courses in the different concentration areas. What first-year MBA grade point average would the two of you, as faculty members, define as indicating a successful first year?"

Hector: "Given the breadth of those first-year core courses, their level of difficulty, and our mild degree of grade inflation, I would say that any of our students in the past two years with at least a 3.2 average would be considered successful in the first year. Would you agree, Susan?"

Susan: "I believe most of the faculty would go along with that."

Wayne: "Don't set your goals too high! Remember, we need at least 60 students per year to even have a program. We probably need to look at the data to see what's possible."

Hector: "When can we get access to the past data? I really would like to get started."

Wayne: "I'll have one of the staff members write a database program that will pull up the relevant information on all students who have completed the first year of the program in the past two years."

Susan: "Please have a copy of the data set put on a disk for me so that I can play with the data on my computer at home."

Hector: "Just send mine through the electronic mail. I should have some time tomorrow to look at it."

Wayne: "I'll get the data to you as soon as I can. Let's plan to meet again in two weeks to see what we have discovered by then. I look forward to hearing your ideas."

Assignment

Wayne McDonald's assistant gathered the data for the past two years of experience with the Westmore MBA program and stored the information in the file WESTMORE.DAT on your Data Disk. The Data Description section provides a partial listing of the data along with variable definitions.

Using this data set and other information given in the case, help Wayne McDonald and the MBA Admissions Committee develop admissions guidelines for the Westmore MBA program. In particular, you should examine the usefulness of the suggested guidelines discussed by the MBA Admissions Committee and consider the possibility of modifying their proposals. Keep in mind that you want to set the guidelines in such a way that the best students are selected and the minimum enrollment of 60 students per year is reached. For each proposal you consider, check for any potential bias in the guidelines, *i.e.,* check to see if there were any unsuccessful students in the past two years who meet the proposed guidelines or any successful students in the past two years who would not meet the proposed guidelines. The Case Questions will assist you in your analysis of the data. Use important details from your analysis to support your recommendations.

Business Cases in Statistical Decision Making

Data Description

The data for the Westmore MBA admissions case is contained in the file WESTMORE.DAT on the Data Disk. The file contains data for the 202 students who completed their first year in the MBA program over the past two years. A partial listing of the data is shown below.

ID	MBA GPA	GMAT	UGPA	UG Major	UG School Rating	Age	Foreign
4001	3.201	540	2.974	1	3	25	0
4002	2.964	540	2.529	1	4	23	0
4003	3.745	510	3.727	3	4	25	0
⋮	⋮	⋮	⋮	⋮	⋮	⋮	⋮

The variables are defined as follows:

ID: Student identification number.

MBA GPA: Grade point average for the first year of courses in the Westmore MBA program.

GMAT: Score on the GMAT test.

UGPA: Undergraduate grade point average.

UG Major: 1, if business undergraduate,
2, if science, engineering or other technical,
3, otherwise.

UG School Rating: 5, if in the top 20% of undergraduate schools,
4, if in the second 20%,
3, if in the third 20%,
2, if in the fourth 20%,
1, if in the bottom 20%.

Age: Age of the student in years.

Foreign: 1, if foreign citizen,
0, if U. S. citizen.

Case Questions: Westmore MBA Program

Name _____

1. One possibility in making admission decisions is to base the decision on the value of a single variable.

   a. Based on the two years of data, which single variable in the data set is the best single predictor of success in the Westmore MBA program (as measured by first-year MBA GPA)? Explain why.

   b. What minimum entrance requirement would you set for this single variable to meet the minimum enrollment of 60 students per year? Explain why.

2. Dr. Susan Thompson suggested raising the minimum entrance requirements to 580 on the GMAT exam and 2.75 for the undergraduate grade point average.

a. Attach a labeled scatterplot of GMAT versus UGPA with MBA GPA as the labeling variable to this assignment. (A labeled scatterplot is a scatterplot where the plotting symbol used identifies the value of a third variable. Use one symbol when MBA GPA is above 3.2 and another symbol when MBA GPA is below 3.2.) Mark the plot to show which students in the past two years would have met Dr. Thompson's suggested admission guidelines.

b. Will her recommended minimum requirements yield the necessary critical mass of students? Explain.

c. From your labeled scatterplot, determine your own minimum requirements on the GMAT and UGPA that will help you better identify successful MBA students (those with a first-year MBA GPA of 3.2 or above) and meet the minimum figure of 60 entering students per year. Mark the labeled scatterplot to show which students would have met your suggested minimum requirements.

d. Summarize the effectiveness of this admissions standard.

3. Wayne mentioned that several MBA programs use the formula score

$$score = GMAT + (200 \times UGPA),$$

to identify applicants who are likely to succeed in an MBA program.

a. Attach another labeled scatterplot of GMAT versus UGPA with MBA GPA as the labeling variable to this assignment. Mark it to identify those students in the past two years who would meet a minimum *score* value of 1000.

b. Will this minimum requirement yield the necessary critical mass of students?

c. From the labeled scatterplot, what minimum *score* value would you suggest for selecting the best candidates for the MBA program while meeting the requirement of at least 60 entering students per year? Mark your graph accordingly.

d. Summarize the effectiveness of this admissions standard.

4. The formula score discussed above is just a special case of

$$score = (a \times GMAT) + (b \times UGPA),$$

where a and b are constants that can be used to give different weights to GMAT and UGPA.

a. What values would you recommend for the unknown coefficients a and b? (You might look at the labeled scatterplot and "eyeball" the best line or compute a multiple linear regression of MBA GPA on GMAT and UGPA **without an intercept** to obtain good values for a and b.) Attach any relevant output.

b. What minimum level would you require to select the best candidates and meet the minimum limit of 60 students per year? Mark a third copy of the labeled scatterplot to identify students meeting this new requirement and attach it to your assignment.

c. Summarize the effectiveness of this admissions standard.

5. Based on your work above, formulate a set of admission requirements for the Westmore MBA program based on GMAT score and undergraduate grade point average. Specify any special exceptions that should be handled differently. Identify characteristics of any <u>successful</u> students in the past two years that <u>would not</u> have passed your admission guidelines. Also identify characteristics of any <u>unsuccessful</u> students in the past two years that <u>would</u> have passed your admission guidelines.

6. Summarize the effectiveness of your proposed admissions standards.

7. Discuss any other variables not included in this data set that might be potentially useful in making admissions decisions.